T0305672

"This book should be of particular interest to scholars of cross-cultural management as it contrasts the networking behaviour of employees from two different Asian cultures – China and Pakistan. The context is the working environment of China-Pakistan Economic Corridor projects. Examining the networking behavior of host and home country employees, the authors provide valuable insights on the cultural factors which either facilitate or hinder productivity in these collaborative projects."

– **Professor Pervez N. Ghauri**, University of Birmingham, U.K.

"China's Belt and Road Initiative is now a well-known topic. This book makes a unique contribution to the growing to the literature as it discusses China's investment projects in the specific instance of Pakistan. The so-called China-Pakistan Economic Corridor represents numerous projects between the two countries. Based on extensive interviews with managers from both nations, this book addresses the role of social networks. The book should be of great interest to those studying employee adjustment and achievement in binational environments. Through the book, the reader develops an appreciation of the role of cultural, and contextual and individual factors in cross-cultural collaborative projects."

– **Professor Leigh Anne Liu**, Georgia State University, USA

"A rare find is how I describe this book. This book provides insightful narratives of how two different cultures and their networking phenomena influence cross-cultural cooperation in China's Belt and Road Initiative (BRI). The book shows how important for leaders from different nations to navigate and adapt their masterplan to achieve desired goals."

– **Professor Teck Yong Eng**, Henley Business School, Malaysia

"Despite the universalism of globalization and even some predictions of Pax Sinica, cross-cultural variations retain their salience for businesses around the world. The need for both the recognition and management of such differences is paramount to success and a key skill for effective leaders globally. Therefore, the authors are to be congratulated for providing us with well contemporary, well-articulated and analysed examples of this important area. This book deserves a prominent place on the shelves of not only libraries but the offices of international business managers."

– **Professor Chris Rowley**, Kellogg College, University of Oxford, UK

Cross-Cultural Challenges of Managing 'One Belt One Road' Projects

The China-Pakistan Economic Corridor (CPEC) is a flagship programme of China's 'One Belt One Road' initiative, created to boost economic cooperation between China and Pakistan with significant political and economic implications in the region. This book looks at critical issues when developing capabilities of cross-cultural management, adaptation and adjustment through cross-cultural understanding and network building from the CPEC case study.

The book highlights the importance of acculturation experience, cross-cultural networking, networking behaviour (*guanxi* versus *hawala*), and factors influencing cross-cultural adjustment, which would enhance the overall performance of 'One Belt One Road' projects in general. It looks at how the Chinese and Pakistani employees' national cultures affect their behaviour while working on the CPEC projects. The book offers insights into what cross-cultural adjustments are effective in creating improved individual and organizational performance.

In an increasingly globalized world in which the practice of working with people from multiple cultural backgrounds is more of a norm, this book will be a useful reference for those who are interested to achieve success in multi-cultural settings.

Arshia Mukhtar is a cross-cultural trainer for global projects and lecturer at International Islamic University (IIUI), Pakistan.

Ying Zhu is Professor and Director of the Australian Centre for Asian Business at the University of South Australia. He has been working as a business leader as well as an academic leader in China and Australia for more than 30 years.

You-il Lee is Professor of International Business at the University of South Australia (UniSA) and currently serves as Dean of Programs at UniSA Business School.

Mary Bambacas is an adjunct research associate at the University of South Australia. She has held senior management positions in the public sector and the non-profit sector, as well as owning and managing a small business.

S. Tamer Cavusgil currently serves as Fuller E. Callaway Professorial Chair and Executive Director at the Center for International Business Education and Research (CIBER), J. Mack Robinson College of Business, Georgia State University, Atlanta, USA.

Routledge Advances in Management and Business Studies

Operations Management in Japan
The Efficiency of Japanese Manufacturing
Hiromichi Shibata

Stakeholder Management and Social Responsibility
Concepts, Approaches and Tools in the Covid Context
Ovidiu Nicolescu and Ciprian Nicolescu

Japanese Business Operations in an Uncertain World
Edited by Anshuman Khare, Nobutaka Odake and Hiroki Ishiruka

Entrepreneurship and Culture
The New Social Paradigm
Alf H. Walle

Hospitality and Tourism Education in China
Development, Issues, and Challenges
Edited by Jigang Bao and Songshan (Sam) Huang

Halal Logistics and Supply Chain Management
Recent Trends and Issues
Edited by Nor Aida Abdul Rahman, Azizul Hassan and Zawiah Abdul Majid

Sustainable International Business Models in a Digitally Transforming World
Edited by Anshuman Khare, Arto Ojala and William W. Baber

Cross-Cultural Challenges of Managing 'One Belt One Road' Projects
The Experience of China-Pakistan Economic Corridor
Arshia Mukhtar, Ying Zhu, You-il Lee, Mary Bambacas and S. Tamer Cavusgil

Cross-Cultural Challenges of Managing 'One Belt One Road' Projects

The Experience of China-Pakistan Economic Corridor

Arshia Mukhtar, Ying Zhu, You-il Lee, Mary Bambacas and S. Tamer Cavusgil

Routledge
Taylor & Francis Group

LONDON AND NEW YORK

First published 2022
by Routledge
4 Park Square, Milton Park, Abingdon, Oxon OX14 4RN

and by Routledge
605 Third Avenue, New York, NY 10158

Routledge is an imprint of the Taylor & Francis Group, an informa business

British Library Cataloguing-in-Publication Data
A catalogue record for this book is available from the British Library

Library of Congress Cataloging-in-Publication Data
A catalog record for this book has been requested

ISBN: 978-1-032-14735-2 (hbk)
ISBN: 978-1-032-14736-9 (pbk)
ISBN: 978-1-003-24081-5 (ebk)

DOI: 10.4324/9781003240815

Typeset in Galliard
by Apex CoVantage, LLC

Contents

Illustrations

Tables

Figures

Authors

Arshia Mukhtar is a cross-cultural trainer for global projects and lecturer at International Islamic University (IIUI), Pakistan. She has done her MBA from Quaid-I-Azam University and MS in Human Resource from IIUI. Recently she has completed PhD study at University of South Australia. Arshia's working career has been associated with insurance, not-for-profit sector and mainly academia. Her academic interests lie in strategic human resource, cross-cultural issues, project management, diversity and inclusion and organizational behaviour. She is also the reviewer of journals, such as *Journal of Islamic Marketing* and her work is published in international journals, such as *International Business Review, Emerald Emerging Markets Case Studies* and *Journal of Islamic Marketing*. She is also the author of the book entitled *Performance of Landline Segment of PTCL* based on her actual working experience with biggest telecom company in Pakistan by providing value-driven enterprise solutions. Being Higher Education Certified Trainer, she has delivered various training on cross-cultural challenges, teacher-student communication gap and faculty development in university teaching.

Ying Zhu is Professor and Director of the Australian Centre for Asian Business at the University of South Australia. He was born in Beijing and graduated from Peking University with a Bachelor of International Economics in 1984. He then worked as an economist at Shenzhen Special Economic Zone in China for four years between 1984 and 1988. He completed PhD on the role of export processing zones in East Asian development, focusing on South Korea, Taiwan, China and Thailand, at Melbourne University between 1989 and 1992. After that, he worked at Victoria University and Melbourne University for 17 years. Ying has more than 150 publications, including top international journal articles and books, in the areas of international HRM, international business, economic development and labour laws in Asia. His most recent books include: *Changing Labour Policies and Organization of Work in China* (Routledge 2021) with Webber M and Benson J; *Weathering the Storm in China and India: Comparative Analysis of Societal Transformation Under the Leadership of Xi and Modi* (Routledge 2021) with Sardana D and Cavusgil S. T.; *International Entrepreneurship: A Comparative Analysis*

(Routledge 2020) with Freeman S and Warner M; *Improving Competitiveness through Human Resource Development in China: The Role of Vocational Education* (Routledge 2020) with Min M; *Business Leaders and Leadership in Asia* (Routledge 2017) with Ren S, Collins N and Warner M; *Conducting Business in China and India: A Comparative and Contextual Analysis* (Palgrave Macmillan 2017) with Sardana D; *Strategic Human Resource Management in China: A Multiple Perspective* (Routledge 2017) with Min M and Bambacas M; *Managing Chinese Outward Foreign Direct Investment* (Palgrave Macmillan 2017) with Huang C.

You-il Lee is Professor of International Business at the University of South Australia (UniSA) and currently serves as Dean of Programs at the UniSA Business with responsibility for the Management and Marketing programme portfolio. You-il is a political economist. His research on socio-economic and political changes caused by globalization and regionalism in Asia has been published with Routledge (Taylor & Francis), Oxford University Press, Edward Elgar and London Financial Times. His work has also appeared in leading journals, i.e. *European Journal of Marketing, Asian Perspectives, Management Decision, Journal of Contemporary Asia, International Marketing Review, International Business Review* and *Asia Pacific Business Review*. You-il's recent monographs include *The Korean Economy: From Growth to Maturity* (Routledge, 2019) and *The Political Economy of New Regionalism in Northeast Asia* (Routledge, 2018).

Mary Bambacas is an adjunct research associate at the University of South Australia. In her working career she has been involved with both profit and non-profit organizations and associations. She has held senior management positions in the public sector, non-profit sector, as well as owning and managing a small business. Her interests lie with people management skills and organizational behaviour. Her work has been published in leading international journals including the *International Journal of Human Resource Management* and *International Business Review* as well as a book entitled *Strategic Human Resource Management in China: A Multiple Perspective* (Routledge 2017) with Min M and Zhu Y.

S. Tamer Cavusgil currently serves as Regent's Professor, Fuller E. Callaway Professorial Chair, and Executive Director, Center for International Business Education and Research (CIBER), J. Mack Robinson College of Business, Georgia State University, Atlanta, the United States. A trustee of Sabanci University in Istanbul, Turkey, Tamer is also a visiting professor at Leeds University Business School, U.K. Tamer authored more than several dozen books and over 200 refereed journal articles. His work is among the most cited contributions in international business. Google Scholar lists him among the top scholars in the world in international business, international marketing, emerging markets and export marketing. Tamer is the recipient of an honorary doctorate, Doctor Honoris Causa, from The University of Hasselt, Belgium, and an honorary doctorate from the University of Southern Denmark. He was also honoured as an Honorary Professor by Atilim University in Ankara, Turkey. Tamer is an elected Fellow of the Academy of International Business, a distinction earned by a select group of intellectual leaders in international business. Tamer holds a Bachelor of Science degree in business and economics from the Middle East Technical University in Ankara, Turkey. He earned his MBA and PhD degrees in business from the University of Wisconsin.

Preface

The China-Pakistan Economic Corridor (CPEC) is the flagship programme of China's Belt and Road Initiative (BRI) to boost the economic cooperation between China and Pakistan. So far, the attention has been focusing on the macro factors of economic efficiency and national interests at the policy level, but the issues related to organizational and individual levels, such as cross-cultural management and adjustment, have been overlooked. Hence, this research investigates the role of social networks and networking behaviour among employees working under the CPEC in Pakistan, along with cross-cultural challenges and the adjustment made by both management and employees working on CPEC projects.

By writing up this book, we hope to make contributions with multi-facet theoretical and practical implications. We suggest that cross-cultural adjustment is more than a 'general satisfaction in the new environment' and requires cognitive reconstruction by adapting and integrating the new cultural environment via social exchange. Employee networking is conditioned to multiple factors at the individual and organizational levels, and employees need heterophilic diverse nationality ties for long-term skills development and knowledge sharing. Consequently, these employees need socializing on multiple platforms, attending cultural and language training programmes, and enrolling in formal mentoring programmes. By comparing networking phenomena among two different Asian cultural groups of China and Pakistan, we have discovered that Chinese and Pakistani employees have different criteria for relationship building, namely *guanxi* and *hawala*, respectively. In addition, the important cultural influence over informal networking for both nationalities might create difficulties to develop cross-cultural networks. Therefore, managerial effort is required to utilize cross-cultural mentors, language interpreters and bilingual managers and mentors to act as network gatekeepers for new social network development in cross-cultural assignments. We believe that the relevant important issues such as employee cross-cultural adjustment and networking behaviour require further investigation in future cross-cultural research in order to benefit individuals, organizations and society.

The Authors
10 August 2021

Acknowledgements

We would first and most importantly like to thank the managers and employees of both Chinese and Pakistani nationalities who participated in this study. Without their patience and understanding, this book would not have been possible. We would also like to acknowledge that this study was supported in part by the Seed Program for Korean Studies through the Ministry of Education of the Republic of Korea and the Korean Studies Promotion Service of the Academy of Korean Studies (AKS-2020-INC-2230007). We would also like to record our appreciation of the excellent work of Ms. Marina Morgan in carrying out the editing of the manuscript. Finally, we would like to thank the UniSA Business and the University of South Australia for their ongoing support of the project.

Abbreviations

Belt and Road Initiative	(BRI)
Bureau of Investment	(BOI)
China-Pakistan Economic Corridor	(CPEC)
China Pakistan Free Trade Agreement	(CPFTA)
Confidence Interval	(CI)
Exploratory Factor Analysis	(EFA)
Dependent Variable	(DV)
Emerging Market Multinational Enterprises	(EMNEs)
Independent Variable	(IV)
Karakorum Highway	(KKH)
Knowledge, Skills, Abilities	(KSA)
Memorandum of Understanding	(MOU)
Multinational Corporations	(MNCs)
One Belt One Road	(OBOR)
Pakistan Industrial Development Corporation	(PIDC)
Personal Social Networks	(PSN)
Principal Component Analysis	(PCA)
Project Management Institute	(PMI)
Public Sector Development Projects	(PSDP)
Qualitative	(QUAL)
Quantitative	(QUAN)
Structural Equation Modeling	(SEM)
Social Capital	(SC)
Special Economic Zone	(SEZ)
Social Exchange Theory	(SET)
Social Networks	(SN)
Social Network Analysis	(SNA)
Thematic Content Analysis	(TCA)

1 Introduction

1.1 Introduction

With the influence of globalization, cross-country trade and investments are resulting in increased cross-cultural exchange activities, economic integration, cultural diffusion, workforce diversity and the emergence of cross-cultural assignments (Ran & Huang, 2019; Shu et al., 2020). Emerging market multinational enterprises (EMNEs) are also establishing offshore investment projects in a number of emerging economies (Buckley & Tian, 2017). However, due to their relatively short history compared to advanced MNEs, EMNEs have not gained sufficient experience in managing several challenges, including dealing with different cultural and economic contexts and ways in which business and people may be managed in these changing contexts (Wang & Varma, 2019). Hence, developing the capabilities of general cross-cultural management and cross-cultural adaptation and adjustment through cross-cultural understanding and network building has become very important for EMNEs' business success (Chen, 2019).

Experts working in the international human resource domain have emphasized the need for EMNEs to select and retain employees who can work efficiently in a cross-cultural environment and are well adjusted to the host country (Caligiuri, 2000). Recruiting well-adjusted employees who can work easily in new cross-cultural assignments is a challenge for most organizations. These employees must have adequate support from their colleagues and organizations for their adjustment to different cultural environments. Unless organizations themselves are also able to adjust to new work and cultural environments, employee adjustment will not be possible.

In order to achieve and maximize economic benefits and competitiveness, many countries have entered into free trade agreements (Mukhtar & Hongdao, 2017). Pakistan has entered into various free trade agreements with several countries, including Sri Lanka, Malaysia, Iran, the United Arab Emirates, Afghanistan, Mauritius, Turkey, the US, the European Union and China (Pakistan, 2018). Pakistan plays an important strategic and economic role in the Asian region and enjoys strong economic relations with these countries (Mukhtar & Hongdao, 2017). China and Pakistan, in particular, have had a strong history of positive diplomatic (Sino-Pak) relations since 1950 (Mahdi, 1986). Both countries

DOI: 10.4324/9781003240815-1

entered into free trade negotiations in April 2005 and signed a free trade agreement in July 2007 (Ministry of Commerce, 2018). The China-Pakistan Free Trade Agreement (CPFTA) (originally concluded in 2006 and came into effect in July 2007) was strengthened through the China-Pakistan Economic Corridor (CPEC) agreement in 2015 (Mukhtar & Hongdao, 2017). As a part of China's Belt and Road Initiative (BRI), the CPEC aims to increase economic growth in the region as well as to create a win-win outcome for China and its participating countries (Hali et al., 2015). The positive outcome of this collaboration for China and Pakistan is threefold: promoting economic development, bridging socio-cultural ties and developing social and human capital (Ahmad et al., 2017).

Besides the benefits and opportunities, the CPEC offers a kaleidoscope of challenges for companies, including EMNEs operating under the CPEC. In addition to the challenges of security and political instability, these companies face several operational challenges in carrying out these projects (Jacob, 2018). Though formal agreements have been signed, operational challenges need to be tackled on a daily basis. One such issue is the interaction between employees with different national cultures (Chen et al., 2018). The effect of national culture on culturally diverse organizations is evident as it affects different levels of the organization as well as individual employees (Pizam, 1993). Consequently, managers need to understand the importance of national culture and its effects on employees working in culturally diverse work environments (Nazarian et al., 2017). In order to build strong cross-cultural collaboration, employees should have the capacity of relationship-building across nationalities for social support with trustworthy social networks (Burt & Wang, 2019; Bader & Schuster, 2015).

Social networks (pool of social contacts of an individual, i.e. the number of people who support work or personal life) as well as networking (ways through which contacts are made and utilized) can help organizations and individuals manage and interact in the work environment effectively (Durbin, 2011). Over the years, social scientists have established theories of social networks and highlighted the role of boundary spanners, actors, social exchanges, social networking and network dynamics at the individual and organizational levels in competitive environments, strategic alliances and international assignments (Ahuja et al., 2012; BarNir & Smith, 2002; Birley, 1985; Blau, 1964; Burt, 1992; Durbin, 2011; Gulati, 1998; Lin, 2001; Sharafizad & Coetzer, 2016).

However, many publications based on social network research have ignored the HR literature (Soltis et al., 2018) and its integration in cross-culture management issues. The literature lacks a holistic approach towards structure (social networks) and behaviour (networking behaviour) in the cross-cultural domain. Network support for employees is integral to their adjustment to new jobs with entirely new work and cultural environments (McEvily et al., 2014; Sharafizad & Coetzer, 2016). According to Pustovit (2020), further research is required to determine the cultural influence of different countries on the development of ties among employees, and consequently adequate adjustment being implemented. Essentially, in-depth investigation is required to determine the role of contextual factors in cross-cultural assignments and provide clarity on the role of culture, individual characteristics and behaviours affecting these networking behaviours and structures simultaneously.

In light of the above, researchers need to visualize the role of different types of social networks and their impact on organizational performance parameters in order to understand the combined effect of structural and behavioural aspects of social networks. Furthermore, the influence of employees' national cultures on social network development and networking and the effect on cross-cultural adjustment of employees require further investigation. Researchers need to understand the fixed (e.g. based on innate traits or attributes) versus malleable (e.g. learned through effort in new culture) views of people with regard to networking (Kuwabara et al., 2020). Though some research has been undertaken on the mutual collaboration and mutual detrimental effects of network types and networking behaviours (McEvily et al., 2014; Soda & Zaheer, 2012), these aspects need to be understood in detail at all levels of cross-cultural management. The cost of premature return of an expatriate due to poor adjustment in new assignments can be as high as US$198,000, and termination of an international assignment is disastrous for cross-cultural projects (Wang & Varma, 2019). It is thus important to investigate employee adjustment for the sake of the success of multi-million-dollar CPEC projects.

1.2 Research Issues and Questions

This book addresses the aforementioned issues using a mixed method approach in order to gain a comprehensive understanding. In particular, this study identifies the types and importance of social networks, and networking behaviours among both Chinese and Pakistani employees working in projects under the CPEC. The role of cultural, contextual and individual factors influencing employee adjustment and achievement of certain outcomes has been explored. Moreover, the role of employee adjustment in the achievement of positive outcomes, such as communication satisfaction, project performance goals and conflict management, has also been analysed.

As a result of this mixed method research, this research offers valuable insights into cross-cultural management studies as it compares networking behaviour across the two different Asian cultures of China and Pakistan within the working environment of the CPEC projects. It is hoped that the fragmented social network literature will be enriched by bridging the gap between the structural and behavioural views of networks from the separate perspectives of host and home country employees, and a measurement of social network characteristics and networking behaviour. The underpinning social exchange and social network theories will also be enriched by highlighting condition-driven networking behaviour and employee cognitive reconstruction in a cross-cultural setting.

The main aim of this book is to identify the role of social networks and networking behaviours among both Chinese and Pakistani employees working within the CPEC projects in Pakistan and the effect on employee adjustment and project outcomes in the cross-cultural work environment. This research focuses on companies in the energy, infrastructure (public sector development, transport and construction) and telecom sector of the CPEC in which Chinese and Pakistani employees are working together. More specifically, this research has four major aims:

- Identify and explore how employees' national cultures affect their behaviours while working in these projects;
- Identify the commonalities and differences between both countries' social networking processes and the adjustments which are required in these social networks for employees to effectively interact in a cross-cultural work environment;
- Establish how organizations enable individuals engaging in cross-cultural interaction to be effective and to achieve positive outcomes, as well as the role of social networks and networking in cross-cultural adjustment; and
- Understand the influence of employee adjustment and social networking on project outcomes in cross-cultural work environment.

Given the significance of this research, the relevant research questions are developed in line with four specific aims of this research listed earlier.

Regarding the first aim of this research, the two key questions are:

RQ1: How do different national cultures (Pakistani and Chinese) affect employees' interaction at workplace under the CPEC?

RQ2: How do different national cultures (Pakistani and Chinese) affect employee social networking behaviours?

Regarding the second aim, further two key questions are:

RQ3: What types of social networks and networking behaviours do prevail among employees working within the CPEC projects?

RQ4: How do social networks and networking behaviour affect the cross-cultural adjustment of employees?

Regarding the third aim, another two key questions are:

RQ5: How do organizations enable individuals engaging in cross-cultural interaction to be effective and to achieve positive outcomes?

RQ7: What is the role of social networks and networking in cross-cultural adjustment?

Lastly, the fourth aim answers the research question:

RQ6: What are the impacts of employee adjustment and social networking on achieving project outcomes?

By achieving the above aims and tackling the research questions, this book provides some meaningful implications for policy and management practices; it identifies network patterns and behaviours among both Chinese and Pakistani employees working within the projects of the CPEC. The social and behavioural adjustments, modifications and adaptations made by both Chinese and Pakistani employees are crucial for working together in a cross-cultural work environment (Black & Stephens, 1989; Chen et al., 2014; Koveshnikov et al., 2014). The role of these social networks and networking behaviours in employee adjustment are analysed along with personal and contextual factors, such as previous international experience, cross-cultural language capability, cross-cultural training and organizational support. This research is made empirically significant by the presence of networking activities which are currently prevailing in the CPEC projects, formal and informal support of peers and colleagues, and the ways cross-cultural employees have initiated contracts and are running their projects with formal organizational support. The conditions and reasons for developing social networks and networking behaviours with mutual collaboration can be demonstrated in multiple contexts.

1.3 The Book Structure

This book is divided into six chapters. This introductory chapter (Chapter 1) is followed by Chapter 2, which provides the background of the political economy in the region with regard to regional dynamics and connected landscape. Chapter 2 also presents a historical review of China-Pakistan relations with the purpose of providing sufficient background information to enable readers to understand the evolution of strategic, political and economic ties being developed between the two countries since the 1950s. The chapter also illustrates the BRI and the development of the CPEC with historical background, such as the development of the original Silk Road and the new Silk Road initiative of the current BRI, as well as the political, economic and strategic implications of developing these initiatives. Finally, the chapter discusses the rationale of this study and the key issues being investigated in this book.

Chapter 3 explains the findings of the qualitative study as Stage One of this research and explores a number of issues: (a) social networks and networking behaviour of employees in CPEC projects; (b) cultural differences and tensions during projects; (c) role of social networks and networking in employee adjustment; (d) organizational, collegial and individual support factors; and (e) the underlying unknown issues. The semi-structured interviews in Stage One provided explorative data to understand the network development in cross-cultural employees. Interviews explored the networking behaviour of employees in the CPEC project companies, the challenges to adjustment and day-to-day work issues faced by the Chinese and Pakistani employees. Stage One also explored socialization, company policies and training programmes offered to mitigate the adjustment challenges. Interviews were conducted with 14 Chinese and 11

Pakistani employees (total of 25 employees) from 5 companies, including sectors such as energy (2 companies), telecom sector (2 companies) and public sector development projects (PSDP) (1 company). An extensive view of the related issues is presented in this chapter by analysing the responses from Chinese and Pakistanis working as managers and employees.

Chapter 4 discusses the development survey questionnaire based on interview findings as well as presents the survey results. The survey was adapted from previous research based on the extensive literature review and interview findings of Stage One and aimed at gauging employees' perceptions of cross-cultural adjustment, their social networks and networking behaviour. Moreover, the survey measured the relationship of employee adjustment with positive outcomes of project performance goals, conflict management and communication satisfaction. The survey was instrumental in generating quantitative findings and identifying relationships across the large sample. A total of 240 valid questionnaires were collected, including 107 Chinese employees and 133 Pakistani employees. The survey also focused on the associated positive outcomes from employee adjustment as well as moderating effects of previous international experience and language training between social networks and employee adjustment on the one hand, and networking behaviour and employee adjustment on other hand. The results presented in this chapter are drawn from hierarchical regression and PROCESS MACRO techniques based on analytical procedures recommended in cross-cultural studies. Hierarchical regression and PROCESS MACRO techniques were utilized in the data analysis. An exploratory factor analysis was first performed to measure equivalence across samples and to identify the structure of indicators. The mean comparison was performed before regression analysis to measure the difference between networking behaviour and employee adjustment across both samples of the population. A moderation analysis was later performed to measure the role of language training programmes and previous international experience.

As the final discussion and conclusion, Chapter 5 provides implications for the government policy, organizational policy and management practices, and individuals' cross-cultural capability building. The chapter also presents a holistic cross-cultural conceptual framework as a key implication for theoretical development. Finally, the final section concludes the book by highlighting the limitations of this research and possible future research directions.

The next chapter provides the relevant overview and rationale of this research in order to ensure a better understanding of the overall regional political economy and the background of China-Pakistan relations and the CPEC.

References

Ahmad, M. S., Asmi, F., Ali, M., Rahman, M. M., & Abbas, S. M. (2017). China-Pakistan economic corridor: In the context of string of pearl strategy. *International Journal of Business and Social Research*, 7(8), 26–42.

Ahuja, G., Soda, G., & Zaheer, A. (2012). The genesis and dynamics of organizational networks. *Organization Science*, 23(2), 434–448.

Bader, B., & Schuster, T. (2015). Expatriate social networks in terrorism-endangered countries: An empirical analysis in Afghanistan, India, Pakistan, and Saudi Arabia. *Journal of International Management*, 21(1), 63–77.

BarNir, A., & Smith, K. A. (2002). Interfirm alliances in the small business: The role of social networks. *Journal of Small Business Management*, 40(3), 219–232.

Birley, S. (1985). The role of networks in the entrepreneurial process. *Journal of Business Venturing*, 1(1), 107–117.

Black, J. S., & Stephens, G. K. (1989). The influence of the spouse on American expatriate adjustment and intent to stay in Pacific rim overseas assignments. *Journal of Management*, 15(4), 529–544.

Blau, P. (1964). *Exchange and power in social life*. New York: John Wiley & Sons.

Buckley, P. J., & Tian, X. (2017). Internalization theory and the performance of emerging-market multinational enterprises. *International Business Review*, 26(5), 976–990.

Burt, R. S. (1992). *Structural holes*. Cambridge, MA: Harvard University Press.

Burt, R. S., & Wang, S. (2019). *Network brokers and bad behavior* [Paper presentation]. Annual meetings of Academy of Management, Boston, MA.

Caligiuri, P. M. (2000). Selecting expatriates for personality characteristics: A moderating effect of personality on the relationship between host national contact and cross-cultural adjustment. *Management International Review*, 40(1), 61–80.

Chen, A. S., Wu, I., & Bian, M. (2014). The moderating effects of active and agreeable conflict management styles on cultural intelligence and cross-cultural adjustment. *International Journal of Cross Cultural Management*, 14(3), 270–288.

Chen, M. (2019). The impact of expatriates' cross-cultural adjustment on work stress and job involvement in the high-tech industry. *Frontiers in Psychology*, 10, 2228.

Chen, X., Joseph, S. K., & Tariq, H. (2018). Betting big on CPEC. *The European Financial Review*. Retrieved 21 September 2019, from www.europeanfinancial-review.com/betting-big-on-cpec/

Durbin, S. (2011). Creating knowledge through networks: A gender perspective. *Gender, Work and Organization*, 18(1), 90–112.

Gulati, R. (1998). Alliances and networks. *Strategic Management Journal*, 19, 293–317.

Hali, S. M., Shukui, D. T., & Iqbal, S. (2015). One Belt and One Road: Impact on China-Pakistan economic corridor. *Strategic Studies*, 34(4), 147–164.

Jacob, J. T. (2018). The China–Pakistan economic corridor and the China–India–Pakistan triangle. In J. M. F. Blanchard (Ed.), *China's maritime silk road initiative and South Asia* (pp. 105–136). London and New York: Palgrave.

Koveshnikov, A., Wechtler, H., & Dejoux, C. (2014). Cross-cultural adjustment of expatriates: The role of emotional intelligence and gender. *Journal of World Business*, 49(3), 362–371.

Kuwabara, K., Zou, X., Aven, B., Hildebrand, C., & Iyengar, S. (2020). Lay theories of networking ability: Beliefs that inhibit instrumental networking. *Social Networks*, 62, 1–11.

Lin, N. (2001). *Social capital: A theory of social structure and action*. Cambridge: Cambridge University Press.

Mahdi, N. (1986). Sino-Pakistan relations: Historical background. *Pakistan Horizon*, 39(4), 60–68.

McEvily, B., Soda, G., & Tortoriello, M. (2014). More formally: Rediscovering the missing link between formal organization and informal social structure. *The Academy of Management Annals, 8*(1), 299–345.

Ministry of Commerce, P. R. O. C. (2018). *China-Pakistan FTA*. Retrieved 4 August 2019, from http://fta.mofcom.gov.cn/topic/enpakistan.shtml

Mukhtar, H., & Hongdao, Q. (2017). A critical analysis of China-Pakistan free trade agreement: Learning experiences for Pakistan with respect to its future FTAs. *Global Journal of Politics and Law Research, 5*(6), 63–74.

Nazarian, A., Atkinson, P., & Foroudi, P. (2017). Influence of national culture and balanced organizational culture on the hotel industry's performance. *International Journal of Hospitality Management, 63*, 22–32.

Pakistan, G. O. (2018). *Trade agreements*. Retrieved 22 August 2019, from www.commerce.gov.pk/about-us/trade-agreements/

Pizam, A. (1993). Managing cross-cultural hospitality enterprises. In P. Jones & A. Pizam (Eds.), *The international hospitality industry: Organizational and operational issues* (pp. 205–225). London: Pitman.

Pustovit, S. (2020). Improving expatriate adjustment: A social network perspective. *Journal of Global Mobility: The Home of Expatriate Management Research, 8*(1), 55–65.

Ran, S., & Huang, J. L. (2019). Enhancing adaptive transfer of cross-cultural training: Lessons learned from the broader training literature. *Human Resource Management Review, 29*(2), 239–252.

Sharafizad, J., & Coetzer, A. (2016). Women business owners' start-up motivations and network content. *Journal of Small Business and Enterprise Development, 23*(2), 590–610.

Shu, F., Ahmed, S. F., Pickett, M. L., Ayman, R., & McAbee, S. T. (2020). Social support perceptions, network characteristics, and international student adjustment. *International Journal of Intercultural Relations, 74*, 136–148.

Soda, G., & Zaheer, A. (2012). A network perspective on organizational architecture: Performance effects of the interplay of formal and informal organization. *Strategic Management Journal, 33*(6), 751–771.

Soltis, S. M., Brass, D. J., & Lepak, D. P. (2018). Social resource management: Integrating social network theory and human resource management. *Academy of Management Annals, 12*(2), 537–573.

Wang, C. H., & Varma, A. (2019). Cultural distance and expatriate failure rates: The moderating role of expatriate management practices. *The International Journal of Human Resource Management, 30*(15), 2211–2230.

2 Regional Political Economy and the CPEC

2.1 Introduction

The 21st century has been labelled the Asian century given the increasing importance of Asian economies in the world and emerging new political and economic powers in the region (Zhu et al., 2021). However, in order to become a leading continent globally, Asian nations need to find their own way to develop and engage with each other; political and economic cooperation is the foundation for the future of the region. The countries have developed their own different initiatives for realizing such an outcome, and the CPEC has been seen as one of the outstanding examples of economic, political and strategic cooperation between two neighbouring countries, namely China and Pakistan.

The CPEC projects have been developed for more than six years with successful outcomes as well as challenges and difficulties. Studies have focused primarily on macro-level development matters, such as investment, progress of the projects and overall obstacles (Faisal, 2018; Fayyaz, 2019). However, challenging issues at firm and individual levels, such as cross-cultural management and communications, social networks and networking behaviours, employee cross-cultural adjustment, cross-cultural training and language training and so on have not yet received much attention. Therefore, it is timely to investigate the issues that determine the eventual outcome of the CPEC projects being implemented effectively. These are the central themes of this book and we will elaborate related rationales in the following sections. However, before going into detail, we start by providing the background of the political economy in this region with regard to regional dynamics and connected landscape. Our focus will then shift to the history of China-Pakistan relations with the purpose of providing sufficient background information to enable readers to understand the evolution of strategic, political and economic ties being developed between the two countries since the 1950s. We will proceed to illustrate the Belt-Road Initiative (BRI) and the Development of the CPEC with historical background, such as the development of the Silk Road in history and the new Silk Road initiative of the BRI currently, and the political, economic and strategic implications of developing these initiatives. Finally, we will describe the rationale of this study and the key issues being investigated in this book.

DOI: 10.4324/9781003240815-2

2.2 Regional Dynamics and Connected Landscape

From the beginning of 21st century, the regional and global environment shaped the strategic outlook of both regional and global economic collaboration (Abid & Ashfaq, 2015). Specially, the strategic vision of developed countries focused on geo-economic and geo-strategic partnerships with emerging countries, to increase their market base. In the late 19th century and during the 20th century, particularly after World War II (WWII), the countries in Europe as well as leading economies in Asia, such as Japan and China, experienced rapid industrialization (Tsui et al., 2017). This growth resulted in excessive output capacity and productivity surplus, with few consumers in those countries (Abid & Ashfaq, 2015; Rahman & Shurong, 2017). As for Japan, although it experienced rapid industrialization after WWII, its economy stagnated by the 1980s due to many factors, such as aging population, lack of market expansion domestically and internationally, economic pressures from the US and loss of competitive advantage in comparison with other neighbouring countries (Rahman & Shurong, 2017).

After nearly four decades of economic reform and opening up its economy, China has faced similar issues of productivity surplus in recent years. Learning from the previous experience of Japan, China has adopted its One Belt-One Road (OBOR) or Belt-Road Initiative (BRI) to combat the productivity surplus problem by expanding overseas investment in infrastructure through regional integration with the developing economies of Asia, Africa, Europe and Latin America (Khan, 2021; Zhu et al., 2021). Regional cooperation was deemed essential with South Asian developing economies such as Bangladesh, Nepal, Pakistan and Sri Lanka, as well as India to a certain degree (Jacob, 2018; Zhu et al., 2021). Besides market expansion, the major objectives of addressing the productivity surplus problem were to (a) connect the geo-economically fragmented regions, (b) overcome the socio-cultural cleavages, and (c) increase political economic and strategic ties in the region (Jacob, 2018; Malik, 2018).

Pakistan was one of the first nations to recognize the People's Republic of China in the 1950s and has had a long friendship relationship with China since then (Afridi & Bajoria, 2010; Fazal-ur-Rahman, 2004). China sees Pakistan as a key ally in terms of regional connectivity and integration given the historical evolution of mutual support in the past decades (Rahman & Shurong, 2017; Wolf, 2017). China has provided Pakistan with major support in areas of military, technical and economic assistance over the years (Abid & Ashfaq, 2015; Wolf, 2017), and Pakistan has provided China with a unique political and geographical position as a strategic partner in dealing with regional and global challenges.

2.3 History of China-Pakistan Relations

Pakistan and China have enjoyed an 'all-season good friendship' since the 1950s (Menhas et al., 2019; Ramay, 2016). Both countries have developed strong military/strategic, political and economic ties that have provided multiple benefits for the two countries in the past decades.

Military and Strategic Ties

China and Pakistan supported each other in military and strategic operations during the Cold War period. The first decade of the relationship between the two countries was challenging due to the China-India and Pakistan-India wars in the 1960s. China was very supportive of Pakistan in both wars of 1965 and 1971 against India (Jacob, 2018; Ramay, 2016). In 1968, China supported Pakistan in building a Heavy Mechanical Complex Taxila, an Ordinance Factory, in East Pakistan in 1970, and an Aeronautical Complex in Kamra, Pakistan (Javaid & Jahangir, 2015). China also helped Pakistan in every field during sanctions imposed by the US in the 1980s, 1990s and 2000s (Ramay, 2016). For example, in 1998, the US imposed sanctions against Pakistan due to the successful development of a nuclear programme in Pakistan. China condemned these sanctions and offered Pakistan help during this difficult period (Javaid & Jahangir, 2015; Ramay, 2016).

Under the so-called string of pearls strategy, as named by the US Department of Defence in 2004, China aimed to build a network of seaports and naval facilities in the Indian Ocean (Javaid & Jahangir, 2015; MacDonald et al., 2004). According to the US, it was China's intention to build military naval defences in the Indian Ocean region (MacDonald et al., 2004). The pearls in this string were considered to be the Maldives, Myanmar, Sri Lanka, Bangladesh and Pakistan, where China intended to build commercial and shipping ports. This move could strengthen China's strategic and military position and provide new opportunity for developing China-Pakistan ties through the establishment of the new deep seaport of Gwadar in Pakistan under the OBOR initiative (Rahman & Shurong, 2017).

The China-Pakistan military and strategic relationship has been continuing and strengthening in recent years. China's Central Military Commission (CMC) members have either visited Pakistan or hosted Pakistani armed forces chiefs, often promoting joint military exercises and development of weapons, such as the JF-17 (*Xiaolong*) multirole fighter aircraft (Jacob, 2018). President Xi's plane into Pakistan in 2015 was escorted by eight of these JF-17s from the Pakistan Air Force, and six escorted Premier Li Keqiang during his visit to Pakistan in 2013 (Jacob, 2018). China and Pakistan have also sold these fighter jets to other developing countries and jointly developed Khalid tanks as a sign of their military strength, friendship and mutual trust (Jacob, 2018; Rahman & Shurong, 2017).

Political and Economic Relations

After gaining independence in 1947 from the British *Raj* [*Raj* mainly refers to the British colonial rule. *Raj* is a Hindi word meaning rule, government, realm or sovereignty (Mitra et al., 2006, p. 336)], Pakistan faced political turbulence and conflicting relationship with India (Wolf, 2020). However, the strategic foreign policies, including strong political relations with China after the 1950s, were important for handling regional and global tensions, such as the Cold War period, regional tensions in the aftermath of 9/11, US sanctions on Pakistan for decades and counter terrorism in recent times (Jacob, 2018; Small, 2015; Wolf, 2017). Over the years, Pakistan has faced geo-political changes and challenges, such as an emerging China in the north-east, an increasingly aggressive India in the east and a highly unstable Afghanistan in the north-west (Ramay, 2016; Wolf, 2017). The dynamics of the region under the influence of positive relationships between China and Pakistan have caused the foreign policies of both countries to be the most logical and realistic, aimed at becoming successful allies (Lashari, 2016).

A border agreement between China and Pakistan was signed in March 1963. Air links were established to open communist China for trade purposes to the wider world (Faisal, 2018; Jacob, 2018). Moreover, both countries agreed to build the Karakoram Highway (KKH), connecting Xinjiang region with the northern areas of Pakistan. The year 1965 was considered to be a fortunate year in the history of the China-Pakistan bilateral relationship as China extended immense political support to Pakistan, while the US imposed an arms sanction on Pakistan and supported India during the Pakistan-India wars in the 1960s (Lashari, 2016). This compelled Pakistan to search for a supporter against India, namely, China, who was fully supportive of Pakistan at that time. Thus, it became obvious that a trustworthy relationship with China was a strong political and national security foundation for Pakistan (Faisal, 2018).

However, the China-Pakistan relationship has also faced criticism internationally, mainly from the West and India. According to Fayyaz (2019), China was seen as an opportunist in taking advantage of the rivalry between India and Pakistan. China considered India to be a 'strategic rival' and, being a strong ally of Pakistan since 1963, China could use Pakistan to tackle the common enemy (Fayyaz, 2019). The strong China-Pakistan alliance has curtailed the influence of India, the US the former Soviet Union and currently Russia in the region (Lashari, 2016; Wolf, 2020). According to Brzezinski (1997), through its relationship with Pakistan, China would be able to offset "India's inclination to cooperate with Russia in regard to Afghanistan and Central Asia" (p. 186). The geo-political relations between Pakistan and China in general, and the current project of the CPEC in particular, have been dealt with scepticism by India and the US and have caused their concerns (Abid & Ashfaq, 2015; Malik, 2018; Ramay, 2016).

Despite scepticism and insecure neighbouring countries, China and Pakistan have consolidated their political and economic relations. The China-Pakistan Joint Committee of Economy, Trade and Technology was set up in October 1982 to promote trade and technology and strengthen the economic relationship between the two countries (Azeemi, 2007). Under President Hu Jintao's 'Good Neighbour Policy' in 2003, China aimed for peaceful development in the region with cooperation among neighbouring countries. China has thus turned its nearest regions into a regional trade hub (Abid & Ashfaq, 2015). In April 2005, the 'China-Pakistan Treaty of Friendship and Cooperation and Good Neighbourly Relations' was signed (People's Daily Online, 2005). Both countries agreed that 'neither party will join any alliance or bloc which infringes upon the sovereignty, security and territorial integrity' of either nation (Faisal, 2018). Moreover, to enhance bilateral trade, both countries made a currency-swap agreement for trade in local currencies in 2011. In order to promote further trade and economic collaboration, China required a deep seaport to reach the gulf and other Middle

Eastern countries. The deep seaport of Gwadar in Pakistan remained neglected for years and in January 2013, Pakistan's government transferred the rights of Gwadar Port to a Chinese company to develop and promote trade in the region (Arshad & Haidong, 2017). Gwadar Port is situated in the Baluchistan province of Pakistan, the least developed area of the country, ranked fourth in productivity and the lowest priority for economic development during Pakistan's previous political regimes (Menhas et al., 2019). By transferring the development rights for Gwadar Port to China, Pakistan aimed to utilize the benefits of trade across the globe and enjoy a strong strategic position for bilateral relationships. In July 2013, an agreement was signed as the "Common Vision for Deepening China-Pakistan Strategic Cooperative Partnership in the New Era" (Ministry of Foreign Affairs, 2013). As a result, Pakistan granted the licence to the Bank of China to open its first branch in Pakistan in March 2017 (Faisal, 2018). This advancement further enhanced the economic facet of the relationship and strengthened the strategic partnership.

According to Hartpence (2011), Pakistan is a significant ally from China's perspective in multiple ways in order to achieve:

- Strategic linkage between the maritime outlet of the Strait of Hormouz and the Persian Gulf to support 20 per cent of the global oil trade.
- A buffer against Indian hegemonic aspirations.
- Peace in Afghanistan, which is integral to regional connectivity and hampers the influence of extremism from Afghanistan in China's Xinjiang province.
- A peaceful South Asian region with the Pakistan-India economic partnership as an element of economic connectivity.

In short, both countries need each other to tackle strategic and economic issues and to build strong ties to address regional and global challenges.

2.4 The Belt-Road Initiative (BRI) and the Development of the CPEC

Background

The BRI, also known as the OBOR (One Belt, One Road) initiative, is a huge infrastructural programme for China's connectivity with other parts of the world, including Asia, Africa, Europe and Latin America (Khan, 2021; Zhu et al., 2021). In terms of the BRI, China aims to develop land, sea and transcontinental communication and transportation projects in these continents to achieve majors goals of trade and regional connectivity, financial integration, cultural integration (people-to-people bonds) and policy coordination (Malik, 2018). Although the idea of connectivity flourished as 'Silk Road' projects in initial Chinese dynasties, with the Chinese Communist party currently in rule, the idea was to develop a more workable regional connectivity network through which all participating countries could flourish (Wolf, 2020).

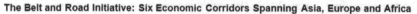

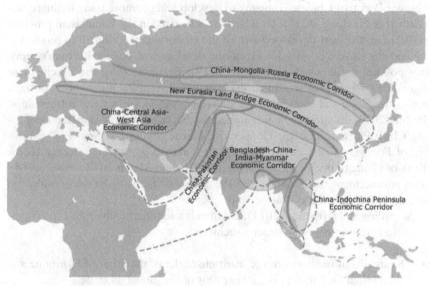

Figure 2.1 The Belt and Road's Economic Corridors
Source: Authors' modification based on Hillman (2018) and Rahman (2020).

During the Han Dynasty, in around the 2nd century BC, Zhang Qian, an imperial envoy and diplomat, created an overland route called the 'Silk Road' (Rahman, 2020). The route ran from Xian city to West Africa and ended in South Europe, linking three continents: Asia, Africa and Europe. Travellers, including tourists, traders, pilgrims and diplomats used this route through the mountainous region of Longshan, the Hexi corridor, the Yumenguan, and Yangguan Passes, Xinjiang, the Pamir Plateau, Central-West-South Asia, Africa and Southern Europe. The route connected the critical areas of today's countries such as China, India, Afghanistan, Iran, Central Asia, Turkey, Iraq, Syria, Egypt and Italy (Rahman, 2020). The route served as a connection between East and West, as well as a thousand-year's old pathway for the exchange of culture, religion, commodities and politics among civilizations of China, India, Mesopotamia, Greece and Rome (Jiang, 2018). The maritime Silk Road was also a dynamic network for cultural exchange and trade between China's south-eastern coastal areas and nations of Southeast Asia, South Asia, Europe and Africa. At the time, sea routes were the main means of transport to export tea and silk from China, whereby Chinese merchants used to bring back spices, stones, silver and other materials to China (Rahman, 2020; Muzapu et al., 2018). In 2013, in the spirit of the centuries-old Silk Road route, Xi Jinping proposed to renew the traditional Silk Road by announcing the BRI (Faisal, 2018; Khan, 2021).

Since its launch by President Xi Jinping of China in 2013, the BRI now comprises the Silk Road Economic Belt (SREB), which connects China to Europe through Central Asia and the 21st Century Maritime Silk Road Initiative (MSRI), which connects China, via Southeast Asia, South Asia and West Asia, to Africa (Jacob, 2018). To date, six economic corridors have been created, including the China-Mongolia-Russia Economic Corridor (CMREC), China-Central Asia Economic Corridor (CCAEC), China-Indochina Peninsula Economic Corridor (IPEC), New-Eurasia Land Bridge (NELB), Bangladesh-China-India-Myanmar Economic Corridor (BCIMEC) and China-Pakistan Economic Corridor (CPEC). Moreover, a Maritime Economic Corridor (MEC) has been created under the name of the 21st Century Maritime Silk Road (Malik, 2018) as shown (blue line) in Figure 2.1.

These six corridors cover 63 per cent of the global population, 30 per cent of global GDP, 24 per cent of household consumption and approximately 75 per cent of the global energy reserves (Rahman, 2020). According to Clarke (2018), China has invested approximately US$40 billion in SREB projects, US$50 billion in the Asian Infrastructure Investment Bank (AIIB), US$25 billion in Maritime Silk Road projects and US$40 billion in the Silk Road Fund (SRF). By the year 2015, the BRI comprised more than 40 per cent of China's foreign building projects, including 1,400 projects for electricity upgrades, high-speed rail, port enhancements, regional development and coal powered plants (Rahman, 2020; Li et al., 2019). The projects aim to boost socio-economic development and regional integration (Faisal, 2018). Moreover, in order to strengthen the people-to-people bonds, China aims to build new projects for education, exchange of academic expertise, faculty and student exchange, scholarships, tourism, cultural exchanges, capacity building in technology, innovation and science, among others (Rahman, 2020).

According to Wang (2018) and Jones (2020), since the launch of the BRI in 2013, China has invested US$70 billion in various regions and nations involved in the project, and trade has exceeded US$5 trillion, demonstrating the realization of China's goal to promote investment and trade beyond its borders and to achieve 'liberalization of market transactions'. Among the BRI projects, the China-Pakistan Economic Corridor (CPEC) project is an exemplary project of North-South cooperation where China, a rising superpower, is investing in developing countries like Pakistan for long-term mutual economic development (Khan, 2021; Rahim et al., 2018). Both the BRI and CPEC represent strategic moves by China to develop infrastructure in these regions for the promotion of regional integration and trade (Chohan, 2017). Although the projects are not devoid of geo-strategic interests, they do aim to promote much-needed economic development in countries like Pakistan (Rahim et al., 2018). Further details of the CPEC project are discussed later.

The China-Pakistan Economic Corridor (CPEC)

In 2013, when the BRI programme was floated, Chinese Premier Li Keqiang visited Islamabad and met then Prime Minister Parvez Musharraf. Both leaders emphasized the importance of a strategic economic partnership between the two countries (Small, 2015) and signed the MOUs for the long-term plan on China-Pakistan financial cooperation, which ensured, amongst other issues, the beginning of an 'unbreakable partnership' between the two countries (Khan, 2021). The idea was to initiate the China-Pakistan Economic Corridor (CPEC) as lynchpin of the BRI programme. However, the CPEC was formally inaugurated during the visit of Chinese President Xi Jinping in April 2015, when a total of 51 agreements were signed between both countries [total worth US$46 billion in 2015; US$64 billion in 2018; US$70 billion cumulatively in 2020. The estimated cumulative projects increased to US$70 billion as of February 2021 (Notezai, 2021)], including the construction of roads, railways, pipeline networks, energy and nuclear projects along with several other projects (Wolf, 2017). As a result of these initiatives, the trade volumes dramatically increased from US$6 billion in 2006 to US$16 billion in 2015 and have continued to increase in recent years reaching US$17.48 billion in 2020 (Chaziza, 2016; Ahmed, 2021). These infrastructure projects have clearly provided significant benefits to both countries.

In July 2015, the year in which the CPEC was inaugurated, a Joint Cooperation Committee (JCC) and five working groups were established during a visit to China by the Prime Minister of Pakistan, Nawaz Sharif (Malik, 2018). The areas of focus included: (1) long-term planning, (2) energy, (3), transportation infrastructure and (4) the Gwadar Port. Later that year, the Chinese Government made the CPEC a part of its 13th Five-Year Plan (2016–2020), as approved by the Communist Party of China (CPC) at the 5th Plenary Session of the 18th Communist Party of China (CPC) Central Committee held in Beijing in November. It was asserted that development of the CPEC was to be based on scientific research and designed by short-, medium- and long-term planning. Moreover, the CPEC would consist of short-, medium- and long-term projects (Abid & Ashfaq, 2015; Small, 2015). This step initiated the alignment of the economy of Pakistan with China's development plan as the world's fastest growing economy (Rahman & Shurong, 2017; Malik, 2018).

Long-term projects (2014–2030) comprise the development of Gwadar Port and connectivity between the city of Gwadar (south-west of Pakistan) and the province of Xinjiang (north-western autonomous region of China). Medium-term projects to be completed by 2025 include energy sector projects, and short-term projects to be completed by 2020 include initial construction projects (Abid & Ashfaq, 2015; Haq & Farooq, 2016; Rahman & Shurong, 2017). Thus, as the flagship project of the BRI initiative, the CPEC aims to achieve economic stability in the region and create a win-win outcome for both China and Pakistan (Jacob, 2018).

Security concerns are the biggest challenge for China and Pakistan in CPEC projects, where multiple fundamentalist groups, terrorist groups like militant wings of political parties pose continuous threat to these projects. Although these groups may not have an animosity with China itself and its employees working in Pakistan, but rather aims to attack the Chinese interests like CPEC as a means to deal with Pakistani state (Abid & Ashfaq, 2015). Moreover, since most of the Chinese companies operating in Pakistan for CPEC projects are state-owned enterprises (SOEs), this casts further doubts in international community,

Pakistani opposition parties, militant groups, and religious fundamentalists, that China will utilize its state companies as a tool to control natural resources, acquisition of sensitive technology and undermining labour and environmental norms in operating countries like Pakistan (Kurlantzick, 2016). Besides this, the state capitalism, where a state owns majority or minority equity positions in firms like in case of China, also faces criticism from private enterprises and free economy proponents that via state capitalism and SOEs the novelty of investment is tarnished, political and economic sovereignty is inhibited in host country (Pakistan) and a dysfunctional political interference arises in SOEs (Alami & Dixon, 2020). Eventually, this state capitalism, via Chinese SOEs, may tarnish the democracy in Pakistan and raise the power dependence relationship of local employees on Chinese employers. Furthermore, the turbulent power-geometries among SOEs and private businesses in Pakistan may arise by increasing the influence of state capitalism and foreign influence through Chinese SOEs.

In some cases, the BRI was also criticized as being the 'Chinese Version of the Marshal Plan', but this conclusion appears to be inaccurate as the main aim of the Marshal Plan was to build infrastructure for emerging markets as well as to restrict the influence of the Soviet Bloc, whereas the BRI does not aim at excluding any other international players (Chohan, 2017; Hali et al., 2015). The salient issue at hand for the Pakistani government is that no programme of this scale has been undertaken in Pakistan's history and criticism has suggested that the "government and its state institutions may be ill-equipped to manage a high-stake experiment under a business-as-usual approach" (Iftikhar et al., 2019, p. 2). However, the Pakistani government has been taking fundamental steps to mitigate these issues with the help of its stakeholders.

Given the CPEC is a mammoth programme (comprising multiple projects), it will provide new markets to Chinese companies for large-scale investment in infrastructural projects (Kugelman, 2018). As for Pakistan, this US$64 billion project has opened new horizons for progress in the field of electricity production, infrastructure development, the establishment of special economic zones and socio-cultural programmes (Haq & Farooq, 2016; Rahman & Shurong, 2017). Although the unique geographical and strategic landscape of Pakistan, located in the cross section of South Asia, has vital importance in the eyes of strategic policymakers, the country is the least integrated region in the world and needs to be integrated in order to build a strong economic platform (Small, 2015). Through the CPEC project, Pakistan can harvest economic and human capital investment for future prosperity (Magsi, 2016). The programme was divided into two main areas initially, that is, energy and transportation. The initial investment distribution of the programme is shown in Figure 2.2.

Geographically, both China and Pakistan share a border at Khunjerab Pass, at which Karakorum Highway (KKH) has connected China's Kashghar region to Islamabad in Pakistan since 1982 via Chitral Division Khunjerab Pass (Rahman & Shurong, 2017). Karachi City and Gwadar Port of Pakistan are also connected to Karakorum Highway via a network of roads ensuring the smooth flow of goods and services. Therefore, the cities and regions located on the route of the KKH will reap further benefits from the CPEC, as the KKH connects those

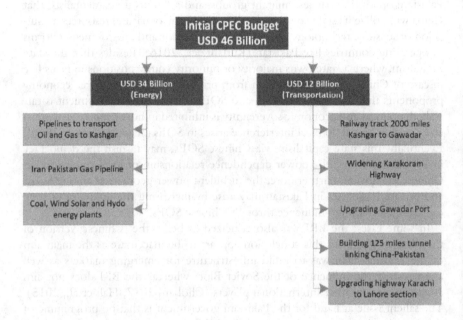

Figure 2.2 The CPEC Initial Budget
Source: Ahmad et al. (2017, p. 30)

areas to Xinjiang province via Khunjerab Pass in Pakistan (Ahmad et al., 2017) (see Figure 2.3: Map of the CPEC project locations).

The lease for Gwadar Port, which is a long-term project and the jewel of the CPEC, has been signed with China for 43 years and 2,300 acres of land have been rented to develop the first Special Economic Zone (SEZ) in the deep seaport of Gwadar (Khan & Anwar, 2016; Rahman & Shurong, 2017). Gwadar will allow China to bypass the Strait of Malacca and have smooth entry to the Middle East, East Africa and the Mediterranean Sea (Khan, 2021). Undoubtedly, Beijing is interested in the industrial port of Gwadar also because of its proximity to the Strait of Hormuz, which is an important water-way to the Persian Gulf and can maximize Chinese import and export capability (Khan, 2021; Lashari, 2016). Since China lacks a warm-water seaport, Gwadar provides a port for the export of Chinese commodities and the unloading of Chinese energy imports, to be transported by land via Pakistan into China (Lashari, 2016), thus reducing the maritime delivery time for the transportation of LNG, oil and precious cargo between Iran, Iraq and China (Rahman, 2020). Access to a warm-water deep seaport means that shipping times will be reduced to between 6 and 10 days as opposed to over 40 days previously (Abid & Ashfaq, 2015; Haq & Farooq, 2016; Khetran & Saeed, 2017; Rahman & Shurong, 2017).

Since the signing of 51 CPEC projects in April 2015, progress is on schedule (CPEC Authority, 2020; Rahman, 2020). Five energy projects were also

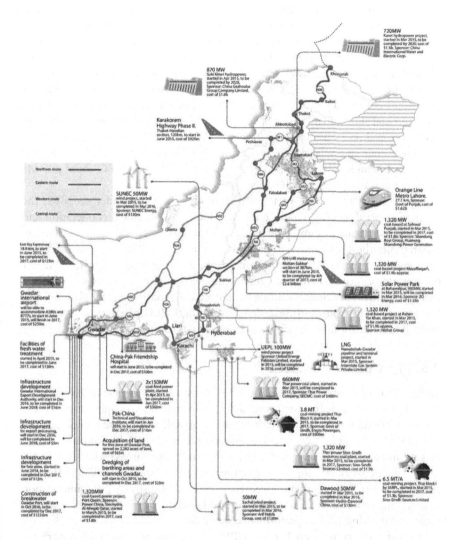

Figure 2.3 Map of the CPEC Project Locations

Source: Authors' modification based on Riaz Haq (2017).

inaugurated at the time of the CPEC signing, namely the Karot 720-mW hydro-power project, the Dawood 50-mW wind-power project, the Sachal 50-mW wind-power project, the Zonergy 900-mW solar project and the Jhimpir 100-mW wind-power project (Malik, 2018). Further energy sector projects were added later, all of which were Independent Power Projects (IPP) (CPEC Authority, 2020; Malik, 2018). Details of energy projects – as a major sector of the CPEC infrastructural projects – can be seen in Table 2.1.

Besides economic cooperation, decrease in trade deficit, increase in employment and investment opportunities in Pakistan, the CPEC will also provide cross-cultural exchange of human and social capital, thus bringing societal changes. Some of the expected changes in society include the compulsion to learn the Mandarin language, intercultural marriages, new cuisines, innovative fitness trends, medical techniques and procedures, and most importantly, inclusion of Confucian ethical values in Pakistani culture (Chen et al., 2018; Majid, 2017). From a social and human capital development perspective, Pakistan lacks a skilled workforce and offers limited entrepreneurial activities. The country is also experiencing a brain drain, lacks education at tertiary level (rural population) and suffers from unemployment (Ahmed et al., 2017). Thus, the CPEC could provide benefits in tackling these challenges.

Given the CPEC is one of the six economic corridors under the BRI, the other five corridors also require multilateral and multinational cooperation and are in different stages of implementation (Faisal, 2018). However, as the flagship programme, the CPEC is a bilateral initiative of China-Pakistan, and successful completion of the CPEC is critical for the smooth execution of the BRI. For the success of future corridors, China needs to establish a role model with the CPEC for other participant countries of the BRI. Therefore, careful planning and full commitment from both sides have made the CPEC progress in a relatively smooth manner though challenges have occurred from time to time.

2.5 The Current Research

So far, the major publications on the CPEC have focused on the macro issues as we mentioned earlier, but the social and human capital challenges of the CPEC for local Pakistani companies and individuals, as well as Chinese companies and expatriates working in Pakistan, have not yet received much attention by policy makers and academic researchers. Some of the neglected areas include cross-cultural social network development, employee cross-cultural networking initiatives and behaviours, adequate employee cross-cultural adjustment, communication satisfaction, cross-cultural language comprehension, efficient conflict management and meeting project performance standards.

In cross-country projects like the CPEC, relocating to a foreign country for an individual expatriate (Chinese employee) is a challenge in terms of leaving the social support system of friends, family and co-workers (Bader & Schuster, 2015). Loss of social networks results in stress, anxiety and uncertainty, thus hampering individual performance (Bader & Schuster, 2015). Cross-cultural adjustment thus requires behavioural change by developing cross-cultural understanding and social networks to enhance individual wellbeing and overall project performance goals (Huff et al., 2014). According to House (1981), when people are embedded in a benevolent network, they will obtain social resources such as emotional and instrumental (work-related) support to combat the routine stress and anxiety. As a result, different home nationals will develop different networks based on their needs. For example, if home nationals, such as Chinese in this

Table 2.1 Energy Projects of the CPEC as of 2 January 2020

	Technology	Installed Capacity (MW)	Location	Estimated Cost (US$)	Status and Date	Benefits
Dawood 50MW Wind Farm	Wind Turbine	49.5	Gharo, hatta, Sindh	115 million	Operational April 5, 2017	Electricity to 100,000 households, employment opportunities to the local people
UEP Wind Farm	Wind Turbine	99	Jhimpir, District Thatta, Sindh	252 million	Operational June 16, 2017	Electricity to 500,000 households, employment opportunities to the local people, generating 268,844 MWh of clean energy
Sachal Energy Wind Farm	Wind Turbine	49.5	Jhimpir, District Thatta, Sindh	134 million	Operational April 10, 2017	Electricity to 100,000 households, generating 136,500MWh of clean energy
Quaid-e-Azam Solar Park	PV Solar	300	Bahawalpur, Punjab	460 million	Operational March 27, 2015	Life expectancy of project is 25 years, expected profit over life of project is US$21.95 million, Clean energy by avoiding 280,000 tonnes of CO_2 each year
Port Qasim Coal-fired plants	Super Critical	1320 (660x2)	Port Qasim, Sindh	2.085 billion	Operational April 25, 2018	5,000 job opportunities to Pakistani engineers and labourers, supercritical thermal technology, environmentally friendly operation, annual energy output is around 9,000GWh

(*Continued*)

Table 2.1 (Continued)

	Technology	Installed Capacity (MW)	Location	Estimated Cost (US$)	Status and Date	Benefits
Sahiwal Coal-Fired Power Plant	Super Critical	1320	Sahiwal, Punjab	1.8 billion	Operational 3 July 2017	Produces over nine billion KWh per annum, expected to fill 25 per cent of the power deficit in Pakistan, employed over 4,000 workers which include 1,000 Chinese workers as of March 2016
Three Gorges Second and Third Wind Power Projects	Wind Turbine	99 (49.5x2)	Jhimpir, District Thatta, Sindh	224 million	Operational June 30, 2018	1,200 new jobs were provided, electricity to local communities
Karot Hydropower Station	Hydel	720	River Jhelum, AJK/ Punjab	1698 million	Expected to be completed by December 2021	3,500 employment opportunities will be offered, reservoir storage capacity of 164.5m m³, tax revenues of US$23 million
CPHGC 1,320MW Coal-fired Power Plant	Super Critical	1320	Hub, Balochistan	1912.2 million	Operational, October 21, 2019	2,500 jobs for local population, National Grid will annually receive nine billion Kwh, electricity demand of four million Pakistani households
Suki Kinari Hydropower Station	Hydel	870	River Kunhar, District Manschra, KPK	1,802 million	Expected completion dates December 2022	Largest hydro independent power producer in Pakistan, generate 3,081 GWh million units per year
Thar Coal Fired Power Plant	Sub Critical	660	Thar Block-II, Sindh	995.4 million	Operational, July 10, 2019	3,000 unskilled and nearly 1,400 skilled workers employed, exploration of coal mining

research, are accompanied without family, they might need more emotional support and thus would develop more informal networks and require more interactional adjustment (Bader & Schuster, 2015; Black & Gregersen, 1991). Others who are accompanied by their family might need more general adjustment with respect to housing facilities or schooling of their children. These needs may help develop both formal and informal networks with colleagues and friends with comparable social and family status. Similarly, different host nationals, such as Pakistanis in this research, will develop different social networks based on their need in a new work environment. They might need more work-related and cross-cultural adjustments based on their interactions with their Chinese colleagues. Therefore, both host and home nationals will take initiatives to adjust to the new work environment within the CPEC projects. Overall, social networks as well as networking behaviour of an individual will help in such cross-cultural adjustment.

The role of social networks has been largely ignored by scholars and policymakers of both governments in relation to cross-cultural employee adjustments. The lack of attention of social network research in HR literature raises the need to consider the integration of formal and informal network relationships in organizational processes, socialization in the workplace, flexible job design and cross-cultural and cross-functional groups for problem-solving (Soltis et al., 2018). These issues form the central themes of this research by investigating how the Chinese (e.g. a dominant group with managerial power) and the Pakistanis (e.g. a non-dominant group but with host country advantages) interact with each other and adopt relevant cross-cultural engagement strategies with possible adjustment. Clearly, it is important to understand the working patterns of individual employees working in the CPEC projects, their socialization process, organizational policies, the effects of social networks and networking behaviour and related cross-cultural adjustment. In addition, organizational support and colleague assistance play an integral role in helping individual employees engage in cross-cultural adjustment and achieve overall project objectives (Davies et al., 2015).

Research on individual informal networks has largely grown over the years in east Asian cultures primarily because of ineffective formal institutions bureaucracy and strong cultural values influencing individual relationships (Li & Xie, 2019). However, individual informal networks research is enclaved in cultural boundaries without their comparison of similarities and differences across borders. A growing body of literature focuses on the unique nature of informal networks in East Asia (Li & Xie, 2019). The informal networks of Korea (*yongo network* or *inmaek*), Japan (*Kankei*) and China (*guanxi*) are rooted in the Confucian, i.e. relationship orientation, influences regarding networks (Horak et al., 2019).

Surprisingly, even similar cultures of East Asia share subtle differences in basic characteristics and roles of these informal networks (Horak et al., 2019; Li & Xie, 2019). Of all the East Asian informal networks, Chinese informal network research gained a lot of attention and overpowered the informal network research of the East Asian region. Like in China the informal network called *guanxi* is very common in other countries in Asia. *Guanxi* is considered an effective way to overcome lack of transparency in bureaucratic process and institutional environment of an economy (Guo et al., 2018). *Guanxi* meaning relationships or personal ties is used as a closed substitute for institutional support, for maintaining strong ties of employees with their colleagues, and in helping them in achieving social needs (Chen et al., 2009). *Guanxi* is an effective way of performing day to day business tasks in Chinese culture and business transactions, especially where work and personal lives are often blurred (Guo et al., 2018). In general, *guanxi* is an implicit agreement between Chinese employees to provide favourable exchanges to their close network (set of ties) employees (Cai et al., 2017; Shi & Cheng, 2016). However, the negative *guanxi* also referred as 'rent-seeking behaviour', is often criticized for its ethical implications like bribery and corruption (Su & Littlefield, 2001). Further investigation has been carried out to tackle the characteristics of negative *guanxi* and its detrimental effects in developing economies.

General observations have pointed out that Chinese employees' working habits are based on ancient Confucius teachings (complex views of moral, social and political teachings given by Confucius during 551–479 BC based upon Chinese values) as well as recent historical influences (socialism) (Fengyan, 2004). The Chinese are bound by closed peer structures and are famous for their *guanxi* practices (i.e. set of reciprocal exchanges and favours to benefit both interacting parties) (Shi & Cheng, 2016). The competition inside the Chinese work teams is not considered good and friends are considered as a source of advice. Given that, denser the social network, greater will be the obligation to help the member of it (Burt & Burzynska, 2017; Morris et al., 2000). There are still mixed pieces of evidence if Chinese prefer 'structural holes' (i.e. prefer to connect to an individual outside their group via a mutual in-group friend), or denser their in-group networks (Burt & Burzynska, 2017). Given the increasing expansion of Chinese economic influence across the globe, future research requires more in-depth understanding of Chinese network encapsulation in homogeneous as well as in cross-culture environment.

Likewise, in Pakistan, there is an informal personal network which uses the 'reference'-based recommendation phenomenon named *hawala* and *sifarish* (Urdu Lughat, 2020; Nadeem & Kayani, 2019). The literature is deficient on social networks research in Pakistani context and lacks suitable term for it. The term *hawala* in Urdu language is derived from Arabic term that denotes 'transfer' – the root H-w-l means 'transform' or 'change' (Redín et al., 2014). In Islamic commercial law literature, *hawala* refers to the payment of debt and forms the basis of banking system (Redín et al., 2014). When the term was adopted into Urdu language like other words in 12th century, the meaning of 'trust' and 'reference' was added in it (Jost & Sandhu, 2000; Thompson, 2008). According to Urdu ontological definition, *hawala* means 'ruju karna (to refer), with reference to someone, to refer in trust, by attributing to someone (Urdu Lughat, 2020). In Pakistan, there is no equivalent word to Chinese *guanxi*, or other terms used in the Middle East such as *wasta*, *blat*, *jeitinho or yongo* that are relevant to network connections. However, the word of *sifarish*, which is often perceived to disregard merit and equivalent to bribery, corruption, or nepotism is utilized in Pakistan (Nadeem & Kayani, 2019; Urdu Lughat, 2020). In India, which shares a long Mughal and colonial history with Pakistan, the term *jaan-pehchan* is utilized which refers to 'Hindi networks' and is used as a mean to 'getting something done through people one knows' (Berger et al., 2020). However, the cultural differences, indigenous local practices, socio-cultural caste system of India, and ontological language differences between Sanskrit and Urdu, are major reasons for interpretation variations between *hawala* and *jaan-pehchan* (Berger et al., 2020; Meyer, 2015). Therefore, this research refers *hawala* as a neutral, rather a positive or negative term as to give reference to someone of another valuable tie to meet social and economic needs, the social tie and a social connection.

In the presence of bureaucracy and deficient formal structures, *hawalas* (personal ties) serve as the basis for providing support, advice and even as a source for job opportunities and promotions to its network partners (Nadeem & Kayani, 2019). However, the negative connotation of *hawala* or *sifarish* prevalent in the Pakistani context, faces criticism as a symbol of corruption, particularly in bureaucratic organizations (Nadeem & Kayani, 2019). Similarly, in the Chinese culture, the negative aspect of *guanxi* could also be referred to as 'rent-seeking behaviour' – often criticized for its ethical implications of bribery and corruption (Su & Littlefield, 2001). Due to a limited number of studies in the Pakistani context, literature is silent on the cross-cultural comparison of *hawala* with similar informal networking ties across countries such as China, Japan, and Korea. Although being part of similar Asian cultural context, it is believed that *hawalas* (plural of *hawala*, references) are not as strong as *guanxi* (Nadeem & Kayani, 2019) and may share similarities as well as differences with *guanxi* in network development.

For the purpose of this research, we refer to *hawala* as well as *guanxi* as a neutral term for relationships and relationship building among the employees from both China and Pakistan. Hence, due to cultural differences, the different approaches towards relationships and relationship building suggest that it is vital to understand how employees with diverse cultural backgrounds develop relationships individually, and how these dyadic relationships transform into networks for sharing diversified knowledge and information for effective cross-cultural adjustment (Zhao & Burt, 2018). Therefore, when both Chinese and Pakistani employees interact in a CPEC project, they are assumed to broaden their vision of alternative ways of building relationships, sharing knowledge and information, and mutually supporting each other for the common goal – successful implementation of CPEC projects (Burt & Soda, 2017; Zhu & Wu, 2018).

Like *guanxi*, *hawalas* are an effective way to achieve personal and business objectives when formal structures are deficient (Nadeem & Kayani, 2019). Chinese are mindful of personal and professional *guanxi* and believe in positive *guanxi* (Li & Xie, 2019). However, this mindfulness and distinction may or may not be prevalent in *hawalas*. This calls for further research for the understanding of similarities and differences between the informal networks of two strong cultures (i.e. China and Pakistan), especially when both countries have strong economic and trade ties after initiation of Belt Road Initiative (BRI) projects

(Mukhtar & Hongdao, 2017). This research thus aims to explore the common-alities and differences between *guanxi* and *hawala* based on informal networks and networking behaviours.

Ingression into Chinese social, organizational and work structure is difficult for outsiders due to strong in-group bonding. However, it has been observed that these *guanxi* in-group networks are not successful in the long run if an 'ego' (person) has 'limited current contacts' (Burt & Burzynska, 2017; Zhao & Burt, 2018). In later stages of teamwork, projects and organizational assignments, it is important that these in-group networks are extended to include people from out-side the network. In contrast, although Pakistani employees believe in the close network philosophy, they are not tightly bound in the same structure (Nadeem & Kayani, 2019). An outsider can relatively easily enter the network structure and work in the social networks. Therefore, when employees of both countries work on the same project under the CPEC, there could be multiple challenges such as differences in language, culture and systems for which employees must make adjustments in the new roles, as revealed by Muhammad et al. (2019). Conse-quently, the phenomena of formal *guanxi* (group centred on an authoritative or bureaucratic figure) and informal *guanxi* (group centred on powerful personal ties excluding authority), need to be studied in the case of Chinese employees working in Pakistan (Chen et al., 2004; Shi & Cheng, 2016; Wong, 1998; Zhu & Wu, 2018) to determine whether Chinese employees use the same concept of *guanxi* in Pakistan and/or what modifications and adjustments are required in the Pakistani context. Similarly, research is also required to explore whether Paki-stani employees utilize their networking behaviour to develop ties with their Chi-nese colleagues and vice versa.

Furthermore, to measure the effects of social networks, the focus needs to be on the individual's network composition (ego-network) and other associated fac-tors such as network size, diversity of network with respect to cross-nationality, frequency and closeness with network partners. It has been observed that indi-viduals are attracted to others who are similar to themselves (similarity-attraction paradigm) and interact and communicate frequently as explained by the principle of homophily (Fulmer & Ostroff, 2016). Nevertheless, this behaviour may create inefficiencies and obstacles in cross-cultural interaction of employees living in silos. Convergence is expected among employees and managers because of the identical cognitive schema (Daft & Weick, 1984) and may inhibit cross-cultural adjustment for employees, especially in the mid-life cycle of projects. The increased exposure to each other's social networks for both Chinese and Pakistani employees can broaden mutual understanding through diverse knowledge, cultural norms and work habits. Furthermore, it can explain the composition of formal and infor-mal network members of both nationalities. In fact, the social network diversity is a contributing factor to employee adjustment due to diverse knowledge and resources from the network partners. Furthermore, both formal and informal networking behaviour helps in interaction adjustment by Chinese and Pakistani nationals. More importantly, Pakistanis' formal and informal networking will also help them in adjusting to the work norms of their Chinese supervisors.

Most of the previous cross-cultural studies (cf. Bader & Schuster, 2015; Black et al., 1992; Hechanova et al., 2003; Koveshnikov et al., 2014; Shaffer et al., 1999) have been limited to a unidirectional perspective of employee adjustment (i.e. process of an expatriate or home country employee adjusting to a foreign environment). However, the research like Zimmermann and Sparrow's (2007) and recent study of Guo et al. (2021), argues that in order to better understand the cross-cultural employee adjustment, it is essential to broaden the scope of study and consider home country employees as a part of bigger picture in which host country employees are also working. Being referred as 'intercultural interaction perspective' by Sackmann and Phillips (2004), employee adjustment in this research will depend not only on home country employees (i.e. Chinese adjusting to a foreign environment) but also on Pakistanis as local or host country employees need to make some adjustments to foreign (Chinese) managers and employees as part of cross-cultural adjustment. It is believed that local employees also bring their business networks and local knowledge which can facilitate cross-cultural adjustment of employees in new environment (Guo et al., 2021). Along with these cultural interactions, there are several organizational and individual factors affecting the adjustment process. Hence, in this research, employee adjustment is a process of mutual interactions rather than a monodirectional process and is equivalent to *cross-cultural employee adjustment.*

According to Sackmann and Phillips (2004) and Zimmermann and Sparrow (2007), intercultural interaction perspective is essence of cross-cultural research, where an understanding of two diverse groups (host and home country employees) interactions is essential. In order to understand the adjustment, it is important to identify the necessary skills to work, navigate and manage in cross-cultural context. Cooperation is the essential component of international assignments, where home country employees must cooperate with their host country nationals and therefore, has to rely on host country employees. As mentioned by Zimmermann and Sparrow (2007), 'Integration' is the most suitable mode of cultural adjustment in international assignments, where both home and host country employees change their attitudes and behaviours accordingly. Essentially, there is a need for more pragmatic multicultural contexts for further investigation of emerging factors influencing host and home country employees' interactions.

An important factor for smooth employee adjustment is a common language. Fluency in English (in this research as common language) on the part of Chinese employees is fundamental in effective communication exchange, improvement in perceptual skills (Ravasi et al., 2015) and understanding of local Pakistani culture. The understanding of a common language, especially a local language (i.e. Urdu), can enable Chinese employees to build their trust and relations with Pakistani employees. For this purpose, language training programmes help both host and home country employees to develop a common mode of communication, reduce misunderstandings and conflicts due to accents and normative values of communications, as well as decrease stress and anxiety associated with new assignments (Black & Gregersen, 1991). Hence, this research also considers the language training programmes and international experience that may moderate the relationship between social networks, networking behaviour and employee adjustment.

A delay in employee adjustment process due to employee conflicts and mis-understandings also hampers the overall project performance, including project schedules. As stated by Eveleens and Verhoef (2010), if a project schedule is delayed and the project cost is consequently increased by 44 per cent, the risk of the project's cancellation is increased by 24 per cent. Hence, punctual comple-tion of projects is an integral factor in the success of the CPEC. Since employee adjustment serves as a mechanism in the smooth operations of business and inter-national projects, it is suggested that employee adjustment also has a positive association with the CPEC projects' performance.

By adjusting to the new work environment of the CPEC projects, employees are able to develop positive perceptions about prevailing communication inside organizations. Employees can benefit from the free flow of information and feel on board when given timely information through communication channels. Employee adjustment thus provides employees with a clear vision of communica-tion avenues in the workplace. Social networks and networking behaviour can also assist in cross-cultural adjustment by employees, thus enhancing effective communications in projects and allowing for open communication among co-workers as well as with supervisors.

Cross-cultural differences are integral to multicultural projects and directed efforts are required to manage any resulting conflicts which can delay the pro-gress of these projects (Anbari et al., 2004). Hence, this research also focuses on effective mechanisms with which to address conflicts in the CPEC projects. Training programmes, especially language and cross-cultural training, play a cru-cial role in generating a positive impact on managing conflicts and diminish-ing the resulting negative consequences. In addition, training programmes and employee adjustment enable employees to develop resilience in the presence of trivial issues through an understanding of cultural differences (Bader & Schuster, 2015; Wang & Nayir, 2006). This approach can create a broader vision in admin-istrative policies and working attitudes of employees from different nationalities. Employee perception of conflict resolution tactics adopted by the management team can thus also be improved.

In the given context of the CPEC projects, effective employee adjustment could result in positive perceptions among employees regarding the manage-ment team in terms of management being transparent, unbiased and imple-menting effective policies in conflict management systems. When employees are well-adjusted through cross-cultural understanding, they are better aware of the expectations of the management team and the way management decision-making is accomplished. This situation will also ensure fairness and provide confidence to employees that settling disputes is a collective responsibility of employees, super-visors and senior management teams, and that fairness in conflict handling exists in the workplace. Therefore, this research focuses on cross-cultural employee adjustment in helping conflict management by developing strong bonds among employees of both nationalities through a better understanding of cultural, attitudinal and behavioural differences.

In conclusion, the interplay between individual characteristics, organizational factors and contextual issues in cross-cultural employee adjustment will be further investigated in this research. Therefore, this research illustrates some real-life benefits of the CPEC-BRI initiative, particularly a number of meaningful implications for companies engaging in cross-country projects with cross-cultural human resource management capabilities. It is hoped that the findings will assist future business operations and companies operating in other BRI projects to handle the issues in advance in an efficient manner. Moreover, existing companies will be able to tackle the grass root-level issues, such as challenges in employee adjustment and culturally influenced work norms, efficiently in order for the overall BRI project to be successfully executed in the future.

2.6 Summary

This chapter has provided an overview of the background information, including the landscape of regional political economy, the history of the bilateral relations between China and India, the development of the BRI and CPEC initiatives and the implementation of the relevant projects, as well as the rationale and central themes of the current research. With the information provided in this chapter, the readers are in a better position to appreciate the reasons, logic and implications of the comprehensive engagement between these two neighbouring countries politically, economically and strategically. In addition, we discovered that the lack of understanding of the challenges and difficulties at firm and individual levels could jeopardize the successful implementation of the CPEC projects. We hope the following chapters can provide valuable insights into these crucial issues. Consequently, policymakers, management teams and individual employees working in the cross-country projects under the BRI initiatives may learn certain lessons from our research. The next chapter will focus on the interview findings.

References

Abid, M., & Ashfaq, A. (2015). CPEC: Challenges and opportunities for Pakistan. *Journal of Pakistan Vision, 16*(2), 142–169.

Afridi, J., & Bajoria, J. (2010). *China-Pakistan relations.* Council on Foreign Relations. Retrieved 24 June 2021, from www.cfr.org/backgrounder/china-pakistan-relations

Ahmad, M. S., Asmi, F., Ali, M., Rahman, M. M., & Abbas, S. M. (2017). China-Pakistan economic corridor: In the context of string of pearl strategy. *International Journal of Business and Social Research, 7*(8), 26–42.

Ahmed, A., Arshad, M. A., Mahmood, A., & Akhtar, S. (2017). Neglecting human resource development in OBOR, a case of the China–Pakistan economic corridor (CPEC). *Journal of Chinese Economic and Foreign Trade Studies, 10*(2), 130–142.

Ahmed, S. I. (2021). Increasing bilateral trade. *The News.* Retrieved 26 July 2021, from www.thenews.com.pk/tns/detail/803196-increasing-bilateral-trade

Alami, I., & Dixon, A. D. (2020). State capitalism(s) redux? Theories, tensions, controversies. *Competition & Change*, 24(1), 70–94.

Anbari, F. T., Khilkhanova, E., Romanova, M., & Umpleby, S. (2004). Managing cultural differences in international projects. *Journal of International Business and Economics*, 2(1), 267–274.

Arshad, M. U., & Haidong, Z. (2017). China-Pakistan economic corridor (CPEC) issues/barrier and imperatives of Pakistan and China. *International Interdisciplinary Business-Economics Advancement Journal*, 2(2), 104–114.

Azeemi, H. R. (2007). 55 Years of Pakistan-China relationship. *Pakistan Horizon*, 60(2), 109–124.

Bader, B., & Schuster, T. (2015). Expatriate social networks in terrorism-endangered countries: An empirical analysis in Afghanistan, India, Pakistan, and Saudi Arabia. *Journal of International Management*, 21(1), 63–77.

Berger, R., Barnes, B. R., Konwar, Z., & Singh, R. (2020). Doing business in India: The role of jaan-pehchaan. *Industrial Marketing Management*, 89, 326–339.

Black, J. S., & Gregersen, H. B. (1991). Antecedents to cross-cultural adjustment for expatriates in Pacific rim assignments. *Human Relations*, 44, 497–515.

Black, J. S., Gregersen, H. B., & Mendenhall, M. E. (1992). *Global assignments: Successfully expatriating and repatriating international managers*. San Francisco, CA: Jossey Bass.

Brzezinski, Z. (1997). A geostrategy for Eurasia. *Foreign Affairs*, 76(5), 50–64.

Burt, R. S., & Burzynska, K. (2017). Chinese entrepreneurs, social networks and guanxi. *Management and Organization Review*, 13(2), 22–260.

Burt, R. S., & Soda, G. (2017). Social origins of great strategies. *Strategy Science*, 2(4), 226–233.

Cai, S., Jun, M., & Yang, Z. (2017). The effects of boundary spanners' personal relationships on interfirm collaboration and conflict: A study of the role of guanxi in China. *Journal of Supply Chain Management*, 53(3), 19–40.

Chaziza, M. (2016). China–Pakistan relationship: A game-changer for the Middle East? *Contemporary Review of the Middle East*, 3(2), 147–161.

Chen, C. C., Chen, Y., & Xin, K. (2004). Guanxi practices and trust in management: A procedural justice perspective. *Organization Science*, 15(2), 200–209.

Chen, X., Joseph, S. K., & Tariq, H. (2018). Betting big on CPEC. *The European Financial Review*. Retrieved 21 September 2019, from www.europeanfinancial-review.com/betting-big-on-cpec/

Chen, Y., Friedman, R., Yu, E., & Sun, F. (2009). Examining the positive and negative effects of guanxi practices: A multi-level analysis of guanxi practices and procedural justice perceptions. *Asia Pacific Journal of Management*, 28(4), 715–735.

Chohan, U. W. (2017). *What is One Belt One Road? A surplus recycling mechanism approach*. Retrieved 30 March 2018, from https://poseidon01.ssrn.com/delivery. php?ID=52306811900 102312300010406408608802403101403907406900306800106509800606906411510202402510301204304710211906506409709608910306804400104501904406802002101007609712412009102001201707412201410106600309807012409300112311712609908510102302 8094069011 09306 6124&EXT=pdf

Clarke, M. (2018). The belt and road initiative: Exploring Beijing's motivations and challenges for its new silk road. *Strategic Analysis*, 42(2), 84–102.

CPEC Authority. (2020). *Energy | China-Pakistan economic corridor (CPEC) official website*. Retrieved 7 January 2020, from http://cpec.gov.pk/energy

Daft, R. L., & Weick, K. E. (1984). Toward a model of organizations as interpretive systems. *Academy of Management Review, 9,* 284–295.

Davies, S., Kraeh, A., & Froese, F. (2015). Burden or support? The influence of partner nationality on expatriate cross-cultural adjustment. *Journal of Global Mobility, 3*(2), 169–182.

Embassy of the People's Republic of China in the Islamic Republic of Pakistan. (2018). *Introduction on CPEC projects.* Retrieved 7 January 2020, from http://pk.chineseembassy.org/eng/zbgx/CPEC/t1626105.htm

Eveleens, J. L., & Verhoef, C. (2010). The rise and fall of the chaos report figures. *IEEE Software, 27*(1), 30–36.

Faisal, M. (2018). Impact of geo-economics on Pak-China strategic relations. *Strategic Studies, 38*(1), 66–84.

Fayyaz, M. (2019). China-Pakistan economic corridor (CPEC): The road to Indian ocean and its geopolitical implications for the India-Pakistan strategic relations. *International Journal of Educational Research and Studies, 1*(1), 14–22.

Fazal-ur-Rahman. (2004). Pakistan and the ASEAN regional forum. *Strategic Studies, 24*(4), 29–51.

Fengyan, W. (2004). Confucian thinking in traditional moral education: Key ideas and fundamental features. *Journal of Moral Education, 33*(4), 429–447.

Fulmer, C. A., & Ostroff, C. (2016). Convergence and emergence in organizations: An integrative framework and review. *Journal of Organizational Behavior, 37,* S122–S145.

Guo, Y., Rammal, H. G., Benson, J., Zhu, Y., & Dowling, P. J. (2018). Interpersonal relations in China: Expatriates' perspective on the development and use of guanxi. *International Business Review, 27*(2), 455–464.

Guo, Y., Rammal, H. G., & Pereira, V. (2021). Am I 'in or out'? A social identity approach to studying expatriates' social networks and adjustment in a host country context. *Journal of Business Research, 136,* 558–566.

Hali, S. M., Shukui, D. T., & Iqbal, S. (2015). One Belt and One Road: Impact on China-Pakistan economic corridor. *Strategic Studies, 34*(4), 147–164.

Hartpence, M. (2011). The economic dimension of Sino-Pakistani relations: An overview. *Journal of Contemporary China, 20*(71), 581–599.

Haq, R. (2017) CPEC financing: Is Pakistan being ripped off by China. Retrieved from http://www.riazhaq.com/2017/07/cpec-financing-is-pakistan-being-ripped.html

Haq, R., & Farooq, N. (2016). *Impact of CPEC on social welfare in Pakistan: A district-level analysis.* In Proceedings of the 32nd Annual General Meeting and Conference, Pakistan Society of Development Economics, Pakistan Institute of Development Economics, Islamabad, Pakistan, pp. 13–15.

Hechanova, R., Beehr, T. A., & Christiansen, N. D. (2003). Antecedents and consequences of employees adjustment to overseas assignment: A meta-analytic review. *Applied Psychology: An International Review, 52*(2), 213–236.

Hillman, J. B. (2018). *China's belt and road is full of holes.* Centre for Strategic & International Studies. Retrieved 20 July 2021, from www.csis.org/analysis/chinas-belt-and-road-full-holes

Horak, S., Taube, M., Yang, I., & Restel, K. (2019). Two not of a kind: Social network theory and informal social networks in East Asia. *Asia Pacific Journal of Management, 36*(2), 349–372.

House, J. S. (1981). *Work stress and social support.* Reading, MA: Addison-Wesley.

Huff, K. C., Song, P., & Gresch, E. B. (2014). Cultural intelligence, personality, and cross-cultural adjustment: A study of expatriates in Japan. *International Journal of Intercultural Relations, 38*, 151–157.

Iftikhar, M. N., Xie, L., Shakeel, K., Jamali, S., Khan, M., Cheema, K. H., & Shahid, M. (2019). *The institutional and urban design of Gwadar City*. London: International Growth Center. Retrieved 30 April 2020, from www.theigc.org/wp-content/uploads/2019/05/Iftikhar-et-al-2019-Final-report.pdf.

Jacob, J. T. (2018). The China – Pakistan economic corridor and the China – India – Pakistan triangle. In J. M. F. Blanchard (Ed.), *China's maritime silk road initiative and South Asia* (pp. 105–136). London and New York: Palgrave.

Javaid, U., & Jahangir, A. (2015). Pakistan-China strategic relationship: A glorious journey of 55 years. *Journal of the Research Society of Pakistan, 52*(1), 157–183.

Jiang, J. (2018). Silk road cultures and the silk road economic belt. In B. R. Deepak (Ed.), *China's global rebalancing and the new silk road* (pp. 15–22). Singapore: Springer.

Jones, L. (2020). Does China's belt and road initiative challenge the liberal, rules-based order? *Fudan Journal of the Humanities and Social Sciences, 13*(1), 113–133.

Jost, P. M., & Sandhu, H. S. (2000). *The hawala alternative remittance system and its role in money laundering*. Lyon: Interpol General Secretariat.

Khan, H. U. (2021). BRI & CPEC: Strategic & economic depth for Pakistan. *South Asian Studies, 1*(35), 217–236.

Khan, K., & Anwar, S. (2016). *Special economic zones (SEZs) and CPEC: Background, challenges and strategies*. 32nd AGM Papers-China-Pakistan Economic Corridor and Regional Integration. Pakistan Society of Development Economists, Islamabad. Retrieved 7 May 2018, from www.pide.org.pk/psde/pdf/AGM32/papers/Special-Economic-Zones-SEZs.pdf

Khetran, M. S. B., & Saeed, M. A. (2017). The CPEC and China-Pakistan relations: A case study on Balochistan. *China Quarterly of International Strategic Studies, 3*(3), 447–461.

Koveshnikov, A., Wechtler, H., & Dejoux, C. (2014). Cross-cultural adjustment of expatriates: The role of emotional intelligence and gender. *Journal of World Business, 49*(3), 362–371.

Kugelman, M. (2018). *The China-Pakistan economic corridor and energy geopolitics in Asia [A blog of the Asia program]*. Retrieved 15 February 2019, from www.wilsoncenter.org/blog-post/the-china-pakistan-economic-corridor-and-energy-geopolitics-asia

Kurlantzick, J. (2016). *State capitalism: How the return of statism is transforming the world*. Oxford: Oxford University Press.

Lashari, M. A. (2016). Pak-China defence and strategic relations: Emerging global and regional dynamics. *Journal of Security and Strategic Analyses, 2*(1), 165–182.

Li, P. P., & Xie, E. (2019). The unique research on the informal ties and social networks in East Asia: Diverse perspectives and new research agenda. *Asia Pacific Journal of Management, 36*(2), 305–319.

Li, Z., Huang, Z., & Dong, H. (2019). The influential factors on outward foreign direct investment: Evidence from the belt and road. *Emerging Markets Finance and Trade, 55*(14), 1–16.

MacDonald, J. A., Donahue, A., Danyluk, B., & Hamilton, B. A. (2004). *Energy futures in Asia: Final report*. McLean, VA: Booz-Allen & Hamilton.

Magsi, D. H. (2016). China-Pakistan economic corridor and challenges of quality labor-force. *The Diplomatic Insight, 9*, 26–27.

Majid, A. (2017). The implications of CPEC on Pakistan in long-run & short-run. *MLA Commons*, 1–13.

Malik, A. R. (2018). The China–Pakistan economic corridor (CPEC): A game changer for Pakistan's economy. In B. R. Deepak (Ed.), *China's global rebalancing and the new silk road* (pp. 69–83). Heidelberg: Springer.

Menhas, R., Mahmood, S., Tanchangya, P., Safdar, M. N., & Hussain, S. (2019). Sustainable development under belt and road initiative: A case study of China-Pakistan economic corridor's socio-economic impact on Pakistan. *Sustainability*, *11*(21), 1–24.

Ministry of Foreign Affairs, the People's Republic of China. (2013). *Common vision for deepening China-Pakistan strategic cooperative partnership in the new era*. Retrieved 25 June 2021, from www.fmprc.gov.cn/mfa_eng/wjdt_665385/2649_665393/t1056958.shtml

Mitra, S. K., Wolf, S. O., & Schöttli, J. (2006). *A political and economic dictionary of South Asia*. London: Routledge.

Morris, M. W., Podolny, J. M., & Ariel, S. (2000). Missing relations: Incorporating relational constructs into models of culture. In C. P. Earley & H. Singh (Eds.), *Innovations in international and cross-cultural management* (pp. 52–90). Thousand Oaks, CA: Sage.

Muhammad, S. A., Giri, R. S., Madad, A., & Ahsan, A. (2019). The influence of organizational cultural characteristics on knowledge transfer across One Belt–One Road: A case of Chinese companies involved in the China-Pakistan economic corridor (CPEC). *Public Administration Issue, Special Issue*, *1*(5), 79–102.

Mukhtar, H., & Hongdao, Q. (2017). A critical analysis of China-Pakistan free trade agreement: Learning experiences for Pakistan with respect to its future FTAs. *Global Journal of Politics and Law Research*, *5*(6), 63–74.

Muzapu, R., Havadi, T., & Mandizvidza, K. (2018). Belt and road initiative: Positioning Zimbabwe for investment opportunities. *Scientific & Academic Publishing*, *8*(1), 18–27.

Nadeem, S., & Kayani, N. (2019). Sifarish: Understanding the ethical versus unethical use of network-based hiring in Pakistan. *Journal of Business Ethics*, *158*(4), 969–982.

Notezai, M. A. (2021). What happened to the China-Pakistan economic corridor? *The Diplomat*. Retrieved 7 April 2021, from https://thediplomat.com/2021/02/what-happened-to-the-china-pakistan-economic-corridor/

People's Daily Online. (2005). *China, Pakistan sign treaty for friendship, cooperation and good-neighborly relations*. Retrieved 25 June 2021, from http://en.people.cn/200504/06/eng20050406_179629.html

Rahim, N., Khan, A. M., & Muzaffar, M. (2018). Problems and prospects of CPEC for economic development and regional integration. *Global Economics Review*, *3*(1), 21–30.

Rahman, S. U., & Shurong, Z. (2017). Analysis of Chinese economic and national security interests in China- Pakistan economic corridor (CPEC) under the framework of One Belt One Road (OBOR) initiative. *Arts and Social Sciences Journal*, *8*(4), 1–7.

Rahman, Z. U. (2020). A comprehensive overview of China's belt and road initiative and its implication for the region and beyond. *Journal of Public Affairs*, 1–12.

Ramay, S. A. (2016). *China Pakistan economic corridor: A Chinese dream being materialized through Pakistan*. Sustainable Development Policy Institute. Retrieved 1 July 2021, from http://hdl.handle.net/11540/6694

Ravasi, C., Salamin, X., & Davoine, E. (2015). Cross-cultural adjustment of skilled migrants in a multicultural and multilingual environment: An explorative study of foreign employees and their spouses in the Swiss context. *The International Journal of Human Resource Management, 26*(10), 1335–1359.

Redín, D. M., Calderón, R., & Ferrero, I. (2014). Exploring the ethical dimension of Hawala. *Journal of Business Ethics, 124*(2), 327–337.

Sackmann, S. A., & Phillips, M. E. (2004). Contextual influences on culture research: Shifting assumptions for new workplace realities. *International Journal of Cross-Cultural Management, 4*(3), 370–390.

Shaffer, M. A., Harrison, D. A., & Gilley, K. M. (1999). Dimensions, determinants, and differences in the expatriate adjustment process. *Journal of International Business Studies, 30*(3), 557–581.

Shi, Y., & Cheng, M. (2016). Impact of political, guanxi ties on corporate value. *Chinese Management Studies, 10*(2), 242–255.

Small, A. (2015). *The China-Pakistan axis: Asia's new geopolitics.* New York: Oxford University Press.

Soltis, S. M., Brass, D. J., & Lepak, D. P. (2018). Social resource management: Integrating social network theory and human resource management. *Academy of Management Annals, 12*(2), 537–573.

Su, C., & Littlefield, J. E. (2001). Entering guanxi: A business ethical dilemma in mainland China? *Journal of Business Ethics, 33*(3), 199–210.

Thompson, E. A. (2008). An introduction to the concept and origins of hawala. *Journal of the History of International Law, 10*, 83–118.

Tsui, S., Wong, E., Chi, L. K., & Tiejun, W. (2017). One Belt, One Road: China's strategy for a new global financial order. *Monthly Review, 68*(8), 36–45.

Urdu Lughat. (2020). *Hawala.* Retrieved 16 December 2020, from http://udb.gov.pk/result.php?search=%D8%AD%D9%88%D8%A7%D9%84%DB%81&posi=offline

Wang, X., & Nayir, D. Z. (2006). How and when is social networking important? Comparing European expatriate adjustment in China and Turkey. *Journal of International Management, 12*(4), 449–472.

Wang, Y. (2018). Belt and road initiative: Mutual connectivity of the world. *China and the World: Ancient and Modern Silk Road, 1*(4), 1–15.

Wolf, S. O. (2017). China-Pakistan economic corridor and its impact on regionalisation in South Asia. In S. Bandyopadhyay, A. Torre, P. Casaca, & T. Dentinho (Eds.), *Regional cooperation in South Asia: Contemporary South Asian studies* (pp. 99–112). Cham: Springer.

Wolf, S. O. (2020). *The China-Pakistan economic corridor of the belt and road initiative: Concept, context and assessment.* Switzerland: Springer.

Wong, Y. H. (1998). The dynamics of guanxi in China. *Singapore Management Review, 20*(2), 25–42.

Zhao, C., & Burt, R. (2018). A note on business survival and social network. *Management and Organization Review, 14*(2), 377–394.

Zhu, J., & Wu, Y. (2018). Chinese private entrepreneurs' formal political connections: Industrial and geographical distribution. In X. Zhang & T. Zhu (Eds.), *Business, government and economic institutions in China* (pp. 165–193). Cham: Springer.

Zhu, Y., Sardana, D., & Cavusgil, S. T. (2021). *Weathering the storm in China and India: Comparative analysis of societal transformation under the leadership of Xi and Modi.* London and New York: Routledge.

Zimmermann, A., & Sparrow, P. (2007). Mutual adjustment processes in international teams: Lessons for the study of expatriation. *International Studies of Management & Organization, 37*(3), 65–88.

3   Interviews Findings

3.1 Introduction

Cross-cultural interaction, effective communication and work attitudes are integral to the success of international collaborative projects (Rosenbusch et al., 2015) such as the CPEC strategic partnership between China and Pakistan. Given the sizable financial investment in the CPEC, the strategic partners are anxious to achieve positive results. From an organizational perspective, the effects of employees' cross-cultural social interaction within the CPEC projects, such as employee adjustment, communication satisfaction and achievement of the project objectives, may outweigh the CPEC's economic impact in the long run. This research comprises two stages in the process of the exploratory sequential design undertaken: qualitative (Stage One) and quantitative (Stage Two) research. The first stage of this research aims to understand employee social interaction (i.e. cross-cultural interaction, networking, employee adjustment and communication issues) affecting the CPEC's success. This chapter presents the qualitative findings of five subject matter experts (SMEs) and in-depth interviews conducted with 14 Chinese and 11 Pakistani employees from the CPEC projects working in Pakistan.

This chapter has a twofold purpose: first, to present the profile of cases being studied in this research and the interview findings, and second, to identify the variables through qualitative findings to be quantitatively measured in the second stage of the research. The research questions guiding the interviews and this study include: How do different national cultures (Pakistani and Chinese) affect employees' interaction in the workplace under the CPEC? How do different national cultures (Pakistani and Chinese) affect employees' social networking behaviours? How do social networks and networking behaviour affect the cross-cultural adjustment of employees? How do organizations enable individuals engaging in cross-cultural interaction to be effective and to achieve positive outcomes? Moreover, the current chapter identifies the project's performance objectives as well as the project's outcomes through interviews which helped in the next phase of research by answering a quantitative question, namely: What are the impacts of employee adjustment and social networking on achieving project outcomes? Since national cultures affect business operations, communication

DOI: 10.4324/9781003240815-3

and management practices (Hall & Hall, 1989), understanding the culture of employees, their working attitudes, socialization and networking, approaches in the CPEC projects will give insights into cultural similarities and differences. These cultural similarities and differences along with organizational policies and culturally influenced networking approaches will further affect employee adjustment and CPEC business operations.

The current chapter comprises three sections. Section 3.2 presents the process of data collection and the profiles of the targeted companies and individuals. Section 3.3 discusses the procedure of data analysis. Section 3.4 presents the findings of the interviews. Based on the findings, the discussion of the relevant outcomes and implications is presented in Section 3.5, followed by a summary in Section 3.6.

3.2 Data Collection and Profiles of the Companies and Individuals

Semi-structured interviews were conducted with employees of both nationalities, to obtain their views of networking processes, adjustment challenges and relevant actions. Semi-structured interviews allow multiple benefits; they allow flexibility as well as standardization through a mix of both open- and close-ended questions (Adler & Clark, 2014). The questions can be modified on the basis of the responses of the interviewees. Semi-structured interview questions also provide the opportunity for time management (Brinkmann, 2014). Moreover, this method allows the interviewer to maintain focus by improving validity and reliability (Patton, 1990; Yin, 2009). In this research, semi-structured interviews provided first-hand insights regarding network development and adjustment processes by employees of both nationalities. The interview guide as shown in Appendix 1, was developed on the basis of the research questions of the study and included potential areas to be explored, comprising but not limited to networking phenomena, development of social networks, adjustment initiatives and challenges. The interview guide also included probes to elicit greater insights from respondents.

The respondents/employees were working in different sectors of CPEC projects in Pakistan, thus, providing insights into networking phenomena across sectors. The data was collected from companies in energy, telecom and public sector development projects (PSDP) under the CPEC in Pakistan (see Table 3.1 for company profiles). Different sectors were selected to ensure operational heterogeneity in the study (Robinson, 2014). The list of companies was obtained from CPEC: Centre of Excellence in Islamabad, the policy development research and governance institute under the Government of Pakistan. Companies were selected on the basis of four relevant criteria, namely, ownership, operations, nationality of employees and location of projects. Selected companies were either owned by Chinese companies or under joint Chinese and Pakistani ownership. Chinese and Pakistani employees were working together in these companies. Data was collected from companies located in Islamabad and Karachi in Pakistan, as head

Table 3.1 Profile of the Companies Studied

Company ID*	Company Description	City	Number of Employees	Industry	Criteria for Selection
P1	Public Sector Development Project Company 1	Islamabad	35	Social sector	1) Joint ownership by the Chinese and Pakistani governments or at least by one country.
E1	Leading Energy Company 1	Karachi	2,800	Energy	
E2	Leading Energy Company 2	Karachi	5,600	Energy	2) Work in progress (WIP) operations.
T1	Leading Telecom Company 1	Islamabad	4500	Telecom	
T2	Leading Telecom Company 2	Islamabad	3,000	Telecom	3) Both Chinese and Pakistani employees working together. 4) Place of projects in Pakistan

*Company names are coded to protect the anonymity of companies. The consent form submitted to employees stated that the identity of employees and companies would not be revealed.

offices of the telecom companies were in Islamabad and most of the energy sector projects were running in Karachi. See Table 3.1 for details.

Employee Interviews

In Stage One of the research, two rounds of investigative activities were carried out. In the first round, pilot testing was conducted in October 2018, with comparable respondents working in the energy and telecom sector. Pilot testing checked the nature and comprehension of questions to be used in the interviews. The pilot testing checked the language comprehension of questions by both nationalities, ease of understanding, adequate response and duration of the interview (Dikko, 2016). In total, six interviews (three Chinese and three Pakistani) were conducted in round one. The respondents were in managerial and employee roles. The employees were working in operations, HR and IT departments. The average age of the employees was 38 years and the average tenure in the current organization was 3 years. The interviews lasted for approximately one hour. Some of the questions were modified and rephrased on the basis of understanding and nature of the project in which these employees were working (Kim, 2011).

The second round of interviews was conducted from November 2018 to June 2019 with 14 Chinese and 11 Pakistani employees (total 25 employees) (see Table 3.2 for employee profiles). Interviews explored employee experiences and perceptions in the areas of networking and adjustment issues. The interviews

Table 3.2 Profile of Qualitative Study Respondents

Employee ID	Gender	Age	Nationality	Sector/ Area	No. of years working in company	Previous international work experience	Pre-departure Training/ Orientation Training
P1P1	M	42	Pakistani	PSDP	10 years	3 years	Yes
P1C1	M	40	Chinese	PSDP	6 years	8 years	Yes
P1C2	F	35	Chinese	PSDP	4 years	3 years	Yes
P1C3	M	38	Chinese	PSDP	3 years	10 years	Yes
E1P1	M	31	Pakistani	Energy	5months	0	Yes, in China
E1C1	M	38	Chinese	Energy	3.2 years	0	Yes
E2P1	M	33	Pakistani	Energy	6 months	0	Yes, in China
E2P2	M	26	Pakistani	Energy	2 years	0	Yes, in China
E2P3	M	26	Pakistani	Energy	2 years	0	Yes, in China
E2C1	M	37	Chinese	Energy	2.3 years	0	Yes
E2C2	M	34	Chinese	Energy	3 years	0	Yes
E2C3	M	26	Chinese	Energy	2 years	0	Yes
T1P1	F	26	Pakistani	Telecom	6 months	0	No
T1P2	M	44	Pakistani	Telecom	12 years	0	Yes. In Embassy
T1P3	M	38	Pakistani	Telecom	6 years	7 years	Yes
T1C1	M	26	Chinese	Telecom	2 years	0	Yes
T1C2	M	33	Chinese	Telecom	2 years	5 months in the Philippines	No
T1C3	M	36	Chinese	Telecom	4 years	0	Yes
T1C4	M	30	Chinese	Telecom	8 years	3 years in Kuwait, the UAE, Co. HQ	No, only self-search
T2P1	M	44	Pakistani	Telecom	11 years	0	Yes, but limited
T2P2	M	36	Pakistani	Telecom	2 years	0	Yes, but limited
T2P3	M	30	Pakistani	Telecom	2 years	0	Yes, but limited
T2C1	M	28	Chinese	Telecom	5.5 years	0	Yes, but limited
T2C2	M	26	Chinese	Telecom	3 years	0	Yes, but limited
T2C3	F	26	Chinese	Telecom	1 years	0	Yes, but limited

Notes

PSDP=Public Sector Development Project

P1P1= First Pakistani employee from first Public Sector project

E2C1= First Chinese employee from second Energy Sector project

M= Male **F**= Female

were conducted with five companies in the energy sector (two companies), telecom sector (two companies) and PSDP (one company). The purposive quota sampling technique was utilized to ensure sufficient representation of projects and employee nationalities from the selected sectors (Mason, 2002; Robinson, 2014; Yang & Banamah, 2014). In quota sampling, the population was divided on the basis of relevant 'strata' (e.g. age, gender, nationality, working history, projects/organizations, pre-departure training and orientation) and quota controls were applied for sample selection (Yang & Banamah, 2014).

The projects were divided into energy, telecom and PSDP strata. Employees were then selected on the basis of quota controls. The first quota control maintained consistency across sectors for measuring day-to-day interaction between two nationalities (Chinese/Pakistani). The second quota control ensured that employees were working directly in the CPEC project of a company. The third quota control ensured that the minimum tenure of an employee in the current project was five to six months. All the quota controls were used to ensure the reliability and trustworthiness of the sampling method across sectors (Sousa, 2014).

The average number of Chinese and Pakistani employees working in companies in the energy and telecom sectors was 2,000–3,000. In public sector development projects (PSDP), companies were relatively small and had an average of 35 employees per company. Chinese employees were in the majority in the public sector projects. A ratio of Chinese to Pakistani employees was not one of the research strata controls and interactions among nationalities were considered important as a research aim. Therefore, Chinese and Pakistani PSDP employees were interviewed to measure cross-cultural interaction in both nationalities. All the interviews followed interview guidelines and lasted approximately 45 minutes.

Interviews started with respondents' background information, such as age, qualification and designation. Questions were then asked in relation to cross-cultural interactions, training, networking and employee adjustment.

In order to reduce research bias, employees were selected from different operational areas and backgrounds (Luborsky & Rubinstein, 1995; Yang & Banamah, 2014). However, male dominance in technical teams and projects led to an employee selection of 92 per cent males and 8 per cent females. The average age of employees in the overall sample was 33 years and the average tenure in the current company was four years. Only 36 per cent of the employees had previous international experience, while 64 per cent of the employees had no previous exposure to working in an international assignment. Chinese employees were mainly working in supervisory and administrative positions such as team leaders, project managers and departmental heads. Pakistani employees were working as team members, team leaders, departmental heads and group heads. Detailed profiles of interviewees can be found in Table 3.2.

Subject Matter Expert Interviews

Subject matter expert (SME) interviews were also conducted from March 2019 to June 2019, for triangulation and credibility of the study. The SME interviews provided enriched data regarding CPEC current projects and deliverables, as well as special economic zones (SEZs). The consistency of SMEs narrative findings in relation to employee interviews added robustness, depth and triangulation to the study. The SMEs were associated with the area of consultancy for the CPEC, Ministry of Planning and Reforms (MOP) and Centre for Excellence. All the SMEs were Pakistani nationals and had national and international experience;

they had a rich work experience (12–15 years in areas such as research, consultancy, public policy and planning and project management in development projects) and were interviewed in their offices in Islamabad. The open-ended interviews lasted for approximately one and a half hours. The inductive research pattern was followed in the SME interviews in order to explore in-depth knowledge of the CPEC and its projects. The open-ended questions were based on insights regarding the nature of CPEC projects, prospects for the economies of China and Pakistan, labour issues, language challenges, among other aspects. All the interviews started with a basic introduction and the scope of research by the interviewer. Each of the SMEs was then asked about the nature of the work they performed in CPEC projects, and their views about the implications of the current situation. Since the SME interviews were open-ended, each SME expressed their views about the strategic importance of CPEC in their area of work, along with cultural changes and strategic vision of both governments. The SMEs also highlighted the number and areas of projects being carried out, and associated employment opportunities and skills development in these projects. Moreover, in the case of two SMEs, interviews regarding the detailed nature of projects and percentage of project completion in the relevant sectors were carried out, in order to gain a greater understanding of the overall performance of these projects. Details about the subject matter experts (SMEs) can be found in Table 3.3.

3.3 Data Analysis

All employee interviews were audio recorded and transcribed into written text. As SMEs showed reluctance to be audio recorded, their interviews were handwritten. All SME interviews followed the '24-hour rule'; that is, all impressions, interview notes and views were completed within one day of an interview to ensure concreteness of data (Eisenhardt, 1989). As mentioned in the ethical section, anonymity of employees, SMEs and companies was maintained by assigning codes. The employee and SME codes were based on the nature of the sectors and designation to protect their identity (see Table 3.3). Nevertheless, none of the details in the interview responses were altered in order to ensure the credibility and reliability of the data.

The thematic content analysis (TCA) approach was adopted to interpret interviews. TCA is considered an appropriate approach for semi-structured interviews and for identification of patterns within the data (Cassell, 2015; King, 2004; Miles & Huberman, 2014). This qualitative study was based on a constructionist framework, where individual motivations and psychological attributes were influenced by socio-cultural contexts. Therefore, codes/categories were developed in relation to themes emerging from these socio-cultural contexts (Braun & Clarke, 2006; Saldaña, 2015).

The analysis procedure adopted for this study was inspired by the earlier studies of Bansal and Corley (2011), Gioia and Chittipeddi (1991), Gioia et al. (2013) and Saldaña (2015). Based on these studies, 'first order' and 'second order' analysis was utilized from the informant and researcher-centred perspectives,

Table 3.3 Subject Matter Experts Profile

SME ID*	Gender	Age	Nationality	Sector/Area	Number of years working (current company)	Previous international experience	Brief description
SPM	M	45	Pakistani	Telecom and Construction	3 years	-	Ex-project manager in railway project from Lahore-Karachi rail tracks. Signalling manager at optical fibre project CPEC. Experience over the last 15 years as a project manager. Worked with Chinese for last 9 years.
SM	M	43	Pakistani	Ministry of Planning and Reforms of Pakistan	10 years	5 years in multiple assignments in countries incl. China, Vietnam etc.	Project director, GM projects for foundation (2015–present). Advisory board member in CPEC centre of excellence (2017–present).
SR	M	65	Pakistani	Government research	1.5 years	10–12 years	Policy head of research division (development/ urban planning) from 2017. Chairman of steering committee on land use for government policy unit of P&D department.
SC	F	46	Pakistani	PSDP Consultancy	7 years	-	Independent HR consultant for 9 years, senior human resource consultant. Currently working on assessing health and safety issues along with PSDP for skill liaising across Pakistan

*SPM: S= Subject Matter Expert, PM= Project Manager (Designation/Area)
SC: S= Subject Matter Expert, C= Consultancy (Designation/Area)

respectively. The first-order analysis, based on informants' perspectives, provided a long list of codes, terms and categories. This resulted in an overwhelming number of categories with overlapping codes and a shared similarity of attributes with other respondents. However, to maintain credibility and authenticity of data, distilling to remove unwanted information was avoided in the first-order analysis.

In the second-order analysis namely the researcher's perspective, the first-order categories were analysed and comprehended, considering shared-similarity attributes between the overlapping categories. As Gioia et al. (2013) elucidated, a researcher works under the assumption of 'knowledgeable agents', thus the codes and categories identified in the first-order categories were revisited and analysed. As a result, a more comprehensive and manageable list of categories was generated. The details of the researcher's analytical steps for the second-order analysis are explained subsequently here.

As an initial step in the second-order analysis, basic concepts were identified which were related to actual interview responses. Such responses included varied and synonymous words such as *communication misunderstandings, communication barriers, line manager, project manager, trust, hanging out, socializing and language issues* among others. In order to develop a comprehensive and summative analysis, the concepts analysed were then converted into selective codes. These selective codes helped in the identification of irrelevant codes. The irrelevant codes were misaligned in relation to the research questions or were unable to generate meaningful implications for the study. For example, the 'problem solving' and 'in-group and out-group' codes were abandoned as some employees described their cross-nationality preference only in the case of absence of the same nationality presence in the support network. This indication failed to match the research aim of the study, which was to measure cross-nationality preferences only. A mind map (code map) was generated in NVivo 12 Plus to help the development of sub-themes and categories (Edhlund & McDougall, 2019). In order to develop conformity with research questions, the concepts identified in the second-order analysis were analysed in the light of the research aims. Following a process of axial coding (Strauss & Corbin, 1990), the concepts and categories were clustered, and hierarchies were developed on the basis of causal relationships among the categories. The finalized categories resulted in aggregate dimensions (Gioia et al., 2013). As a confirmatory tool, the NVivo 12 Plus was also used to check for missing themes and codes. Auto coding was used as an automated insight tool to generate the codes. The auto codes were checked with existing codes to ensure that important elements were not overlooked. After following all the steps, specific themes were developed (see Figure 3.1).

The first aggregate dimension, namely 'the impact of national cultures and cultural tensions', relates to the first research aim to determine the effect of national cultures on employee behaviour working in the CPEC projects. Similarly, the second aggregate dimension of 'factors influencing cross-cultural interaction and adjustment' relates to the commonalities and differences between both countries' social networking processes. Moreover, the second aggregate dimension also elucidates the employee adjustments which are required in these social networks for

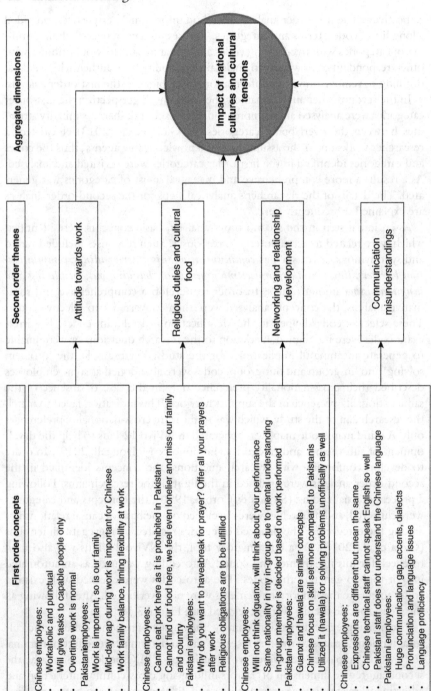

Aggregate dimensions

Second order themes

First order concepts

Impact of national cultures and cultural tensions

Attitude towards work

Chinese employees:
· Workaholic and punctual
· Will give tasks to capable people only
· Overtime work is normal
Pakistani employees:
· Work is important, so is our family
· Mid-day nap during work is important for Chinese
· Work family balance, timing flexibility at work

Religious duties and cultural food

Chinese employees:
· Cannot eat pork here as it is prohibited in Pakistan
· Cannot find our food here, we feel even lonelier and miss our family and country
Pakistani employees:
· Why do you want to have a break for prayer? Offer all your prayers after work
· Religious obligations are to be fulfilled

Networking and relationship development

Chinese employees:
· Will not think of guanxi, will think about your performance
· Same nationality in my in-group due to mental understanding
· In-group member is decided based on work performed
Pakistani employees:
· Guanxi and hawala are similar concepts
· Chinese focus on skill set more compared to Pakistanis
· Utilized it (hawala) for solving problems unofficially as well

Communication misunderstandings

Chinese employees:
· Expressions are different but mean the same
· Chinese technical staff cannot speak English so well
· Pakistani staff does not understand the Chinese language
Pakistani employees:
· Huge communication gap, accents, dialects
· Pronunciation and language issues
· Language proficiency

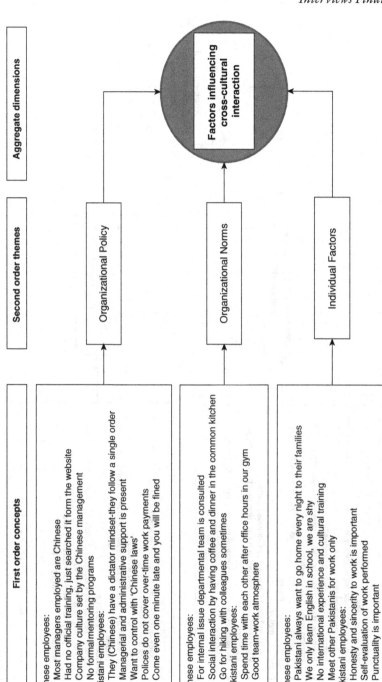

Figure 3.1b Continued

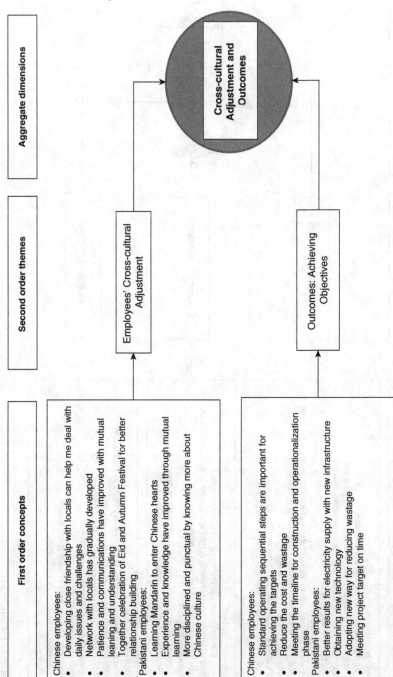

Figure 3.1c Data Structure

employees to effectively interact in a cross-cultural work environment. Lastly, the 'cross-cultural adjustment and outcomes' aggregate dimension corresponds to the networking effects on employee adjustment and consequently the influence on outcomes, that is, achieving objectives in the cross-cultural work environment (see Figure 3.1).

Finally, a secondary data analysis of published documents on CPEC projects was carried out. In addition to interviews, secondary data analysis facilitated triangulation of data. Documents were read in several iterations to explore (a) how employee's adjustment is influenced by their networking opportunities and social networks and (b) CPEC project attributes such as costs and completion timelines. The documents were analysed on the basis of the aforementioned aggregate dimensions and research questions. These documents thus added further insights regarding the relevant issues.

3.4 Interview Findings

Impact of Different National Cultures and Cultural Tensions

Over the last three decades, people have been concerned with the impact of cultural differences on people working in international projects (Nazarian et al., 2017). Cultural similarities among employees of different nationalities have been found to enhance project performance goals (Nazarian et al., 2017). However, cultural differences between employees of different nationalities can also create difficulties and problems for both host and home country employees.

This study observed both commonalities and differences between the cultural norms of Chinese and Pakistanis working together. Essentially, national culture similarities were conducive to cross-cultural interaction and consequently adjustment, whereas differences created obstacles in effective adjustment and work efficiency.

In all sectors, Chinese nationals were mainly working in administrative and supervisory positions, and Pakistani nationals were working as team members, team leaders and in supervisory positions. However, a few of the Chinese were also working as employees at subordinate level in these sectors. Therefore, the generic term of 'employees' is used to refer to all Chinese and Pakistani cadres and workers.

With regard to the Chinese employees, they claimed that they held positive attitude towards work. These Chinese employees envisioned themselves as hardworking and disciplined employees, while considering time as a precious entity which should be utilized to its fullest. As a result, working overtime and achieving goals beyond the expected threshold levels was considered normal. Moreover, these employees considered leave from work to be a privilege and to be accessed in the case of emergency. As one Chinese employee (E2C1) commented:

"We don't apply for leave often for small health issues, for example, in China, if we are not feeling well, most of us won't apply for leave and will still go to work."

In Chinese work culture, punctuality and discipline are important elements of work life, where optimum utilization of time is essential for the achievement of work goals (Baumann et al., 2016; Chiu & Kosinski, 1995). This philosophy was also revealed by Chinese employees in the current sample with a strong sense of responsibility to work, where overtime work and goal achievement beyond the threshold level was considered normal. As most of the employees (over 78 per cent) in the current sample have come to Pakistan without their families, they seek refuge in work to overcome loneliness. As a result, a sense of urgency was prevalent among Chinese employees to complete their assignments and return to China to re-join their families.

Further analysis from interviews revealed that Pakistani employees also had a fair understanding of Chinese employees' expectations and basic cultural norms. Over 96 per cent of the Pakistani respondents in this study admitted that they admired Chinese employees' work ethics (i.e. hard work, punctuality and work focus). Generally, the Chinese attitude to government funded projects was characterized by the allocation of high priority to and the achievement of on-time project completion objectives. At the same time, Pakistani employees believed Chinese employees to be efficient, target-oriented and good in analytical skills, as described by one Pakistani employee (TIP3):

> They (Chinese managers) can judge you very favourably if you are capable and efficient. They are very efficient and good at analysing people and utilizing that analysis in assigning tasks to capable people only.

The above statement illustrates the prudent approach of Chinese employees in projects. In contrast, the current sample revealed that Pakistani employees were strong believers of work-family balance and family bonding. One Pakistani employee (T1P2) reported that Pakistanis believe that 'personal life, including family, should find space for a job and not the other way around'. As an extension of this approach, the basic beliefs of Pakistani society constitute of life as a mix of family, society, neighbours, religion, comradeship, brotherhood and job as a source of earnings and making ends meet (Burki & Ziring, 2019). Moreover, as the Pakistani employees were living with their families, family responsibilities were an integral component of daily routine. According to these beliefs, Pakistani employees treated work and family as equally important and with a sense of balance. One Pakistani employee (T1P3) explained his view:

> As Pakistanis, we have to take care of many things like our parents and our siblings. So, we have a lot of responsibilities and I think this is the reason we need to earn money.

Hence, whenever overtime work was required, Pakistani employees were reluctant due to their concern for an imbalance between work-family responsibilities. Different cultural expectations regarding time and devotion to work and family responsibilities, created tensions among Chinese and Pakistani employees and affected work efficiency.

In general, most Chinese employees thought Pakistani employees were friendly and hardworking but lacked punctuality and high commitment to work. Chinese employees held a low view of Pakistani employees using their leave for small problems. One of the Chinese supervisors (CTP1) reflected:

> [H]ere (in Pakistan) it is very different. Most of the Pakistani staff will apply for leave even if it is a very small problem like a headache etc. I have also discussed that with other people (Pakistanis) and they say we don't understand why you Chinese don't apply for leave when you are not feeling well.

In most cases the Pakistani employees (73 per cent) were troubled by the Chinese employees' limited knowledge of their Muslim culture. Pakistan is a Muslim majority country where religious obligations are an integral part of Pakistani society. A typical Pakistani Muslim honours religious obligations at a particular time of the year (e.g. fasting in the month of Ramadan) as well as at a particular time of day (e.g. obligatory prayers which are offered five times a day) (The Pew Forum on Religion & Public Life, 2012). However, Chinese managers were not aware of the importance of religious activities due to different social and cultural norms in China.

According to the report of the Council on Foreign Relations released on 11 October 2018, the research and advocacy group Freedom House estimates that more than 350 million religious believers in China are followers of Buddhism, Christianity, and Daoism, among others. The Muslim population constitutes only 1.6 per cent (22 million) of China's population and is mainly located in the northwest autonomous provinces (Albert, 2018). Hence, as the Chinese are mainly followers of other religions or have non-religious backgrounds (e.g. Buddhism, Christianity and atheism), they have limited knowledge of Muslim culture. It was evident that the Chinese had difficulty understanding the Pakistani Muslims' religious duties, as can be seen in the statement of one Pakistani employee (E1P1):

> They say, why do you want to have a break for prayer? You can offer all of your prayers after work. They don't know anything about religion.

This statement reveals different expectations about work arising from religious commitments between these employees from different nationalities. Chinese employees considered that religious duties create inefficiencies in work routine and jeopardize the possibilities of achieving daily targets. Such differences escalated misunderstandings between Chinese and Pakistani employees.

Another challenging issue was the lack of easily available Chinese food and ingredients in Pakistan, contributing to the homesickness experienced by Chinese employees and eventually contributing to dissatisfaction and maladjustment. Chinese in Pakistan are prohibited from eating pork and drinking liquor as Islamic rules clearly prohibit both. Under the Pakistan penal code, Hadood ordinance

of 1979 and Islamic laws, selling and consumption of alcohol and pork are prohibited in Pakistan. It is considered a crime to sell alcohol to Muslims or publicly
consume it (Haider, 2014). One Chinese employee expressed the thoughts of
a few other Chinese (28 per cent) in the energy sector as follows: "We can't eat
pork here as it is not allowed to eat it in Pakistan. Our family is not here and if
we can't find our food here, we feel even more lonely and miss our family and
country."

Table 3.4 presents the comparative analysis of distinguishing attributes among
Chinese and Pakistani employees.

Based on the culturally complex phenomenon of employee interactions, it was
observed from the interviewees' accounts that both nationalities believed in strong
relationships in personal and professional life. Social networks, especially proactiveness in networking (i.e. development of connections or relationship building),
were essential factors in catering for organizational-level bureaucracies. However,
employees had mixed views regarding the in-group (within the social network)
and outgroup (outside the social network) phenomena (i.e. social networks composition). In particular, when employees where asked whether there were new
people who had been added in their in-group since they started working on the
project, employees from both nationalities reported that work was dynamic in
nature and the projects were still in their take-off phase. Hence, in-group membership is not stable and cannot be determined due to frequent change in work
teams and worksites. Therefore, the measurement of new in-group members is
inapplicable. Additionally, though employees brought with them their previous
social networks, new social networks constituency was dependent upon ample
time spent in the project.

With regard to the effect of different national cultures on employee social networking behaviours, the result of interviews with both Chinese and Pakistani
employees substantiated that networking (i.e. *guanxi* for Chinese and *hawalas* for
Pakistani employees) was an integral element in the achievement of goals, where
some Chinese employees believed that Pakistani employees had more *guanxi* than
Chinese employees. Pakistani employees, on the other hand, believed that 'social
connection' *(hawala)* was a 'universal truth' and was present in every culture and
workplace. While identifying the characteristics of networking, both nationalities
reported that networking and social networks development enabled individuals
to identify a potential person with resources who could benefit them in work,
personal life or both. Whereas Chinese employees decided the networking criteria based on work quality, performance and reliability (work basis), Pakistani
employees determined networking based on common values, understanding,
trust and work reliability (mainly social and personal basis). Overall, the purpose
and basic characteristics of networking were consistent across both nationalities.
However, criteria for the *guanxi* and *hawala* differ across both nationalities. For
example, the Chinese employees developed connections only after measuring an
individual's performance in order to guarantee the connections were only with
capable people. For these employees, personal *guanxi* should not come at the
expense of work quality in the workplace. Hence, Chinese employees were seen

Table 3.4 Comparative Analysis of Distinguishing Attributes

	Chinese Views of Chinese Employees	*Chinese Views of Pakistani Employees*	*Pakistani Views of Pakistani Employees*	*Pakistani Views of Chinese Employees*
Basic cultural norms:	70 % of Chinese employees reported that they are: workaholic, hardworking and disciplined.	92% Chinese employees reported that Pakistanis are: religious, friendly, prefer family to work and are fluent in English.	91.6 % of Pakistani employees reported that they prefer: work-family balance, human connections, strong family bonding, brotherhood and friendships.	96.7 % of Pakistani employees reported that Chinese are: workaholic, punctual and authoritarian. 23% believed that Chinese are good in analytical skills, efficient and target oriented.
Religious Norms:	Not follower of any particular religion.	Punctuality in religious duties, e.g. prayer, fasting etc.	Obligation to follow religion. Essential part of life.	73 % of Pakistanis reported that Chinese have limited knowledge of Muslim culture and prayers.
English Proficiency:	70% of Chinese reported having weak proficiency.	Good proficiency in English.	Benefit of English colonial influence. Proficiency in English.	83% of Pakistanis reported Chinese have weak proficiency.
Food liking:	Only 18% Chinese reported that they started liking Pakistani food.	18% Chinese reported that they started liking Pakistani cuisine.	Some liking for modified and halal Chinese cuisine.	
In-group inclusion:	31% Chinese reported new people had been added. 54% were unable to measure to measure if new people had been added. The remaining denied the in-group phenomenon.		42% of Pakistanis reported new people had been added. The remaining reported difficulty tin measuring in-group phenomenon.	
Employee Adjustment:	92% of Chinese employees reported they had adjusted compared to when they started work in Pakistan.			91.6% of Pakistani employees reported they had adjusted compared to when they started in the CPEC project alongside the Chinese.

to be more professionally-oriented in their work, whereby personal *guanxi* was discerned on the basis of professional *guanxi*, as affirmatively stated by one Chinese employee (T1C3):

> If your performance is not good, even if your relationship is good, your skills are useless. Even if you think that I will help you just because of *guanxi*, I will not think of *guanxi*, I will think about your performance.

This illustrates the Chinese mindset of creating distinguishable boundaries between personal and professional *guanxi*. In contrast, for Pakistani employees, *guanxi* and *hawalas* shared similar meaning (i.e. developing connections or building relationships), with an unclear distinction between personal and professional ties. Pakistani employees used the term *hawalas* interchangeably in personal and professional life (personal and professionals *hawalas*) as needed. They believed that *hawalas* help in achieving personal and professional goals which either could not be achieved without personal connections or could be delayed in the formal bureaucratic process. One Pakistani employee (P1P1) described *hawalas* as follows:

> In *guanxi* they believe in giving gifts, networking for long term relationships. They try to make their boss happy. You see, that is the same here in *hawalas*. I mean most of our lives are spent in building connections with the people who we think will benefit us in the longer run.

Within the context of social networks and networking behaviour affecting cross-cultural adjustment of employees, the aforementioned comments confirm that the Chinese employees distinguish between professional and personal ties whereas Pakistani employees utilize both ties interchangeably. Chinese employees appear to be hindered in adjusting to Pakistani employees as they consider Pakistani employees from the perspective of professional ties (formal) and network members to be consulted for work only. The differences between the Chinese and Pakistani employees' understanding and use of *guanxi* and *hawalas* eventually create conflict. In general, when Pakistani employees try to favour their personal network employee in teamwork and job opportunities, Chinese employees consider it a lack of professionalism. Pakistani employees believe in comradeship and brotherhood, and hence they try to help their 'brother' wherever possible (within the legal and ethical boundaries created by Pakistani cultural norms). *Hawalas*, according to some Pakistani employees, are also categorized by nepotism and *sifarish* [Urdu language word for undue favour to members of a network, and it is commonly used in negative connotation (Nadeem & Kayani, 2019)] due to the utilization of interchangeable professional and personal ties for long-term relationships developed with beneficiaries. In this sense, *hawalas* can have a negative meaning.

In terms of network entry, Chinese employees try to access the existing social networks of Pakistani employees by establishing rapport and trust. In contrast,

Pakistani employees struggle to gain acceptance in Chinese networks due to a lack of trust. One Pakistani employee (T2P1) claimed that, although Chinese employees tried to develop connections with Pakistani employees, they lacked comprehension of Pakistani cultural norms of networking:

> They would just have a word with you for five minutes. The basic questions, and then expect that there's a connection. They try to rush through it. The Pakistani guys would also do the same. But they would do it in a nicer way (Pakistani). These (Chinese) guys are blunt.

This lack of understanding regarding networking cultural norms further restricts Chinese employees in accessing Pakistani employees' social networks and adjusting to the environment accordingly. The overall response to issues related to social networking reveals that most employees (i.e. 95 per cent) observed some similarity between *guanxi* and *hawala* systems based on building connections and using those connections. The remaining (5 per cent of the employees, all Pakistanis) either did not respond to the issue or tried to avoid it due to the negative connotation attached to the word *hawala* (*sifarish* and nepotism) as discussed earlier.

Factors Influencing Cross-Cultural Interaction and Adjustment

Cross-cultural interaction and adjustment in international projects are also affected by multiple organizational and individual interactional factors. Sometimes these factors are conducive to the adjustment, other times they can pose certain challenges in cross-cultural assignments due to differences in values and norms of the cultures. Organization policies and norms are the key factors for individual interaction in official settings (Konanahalli et al., 2014). While these factors guide, monitor and control employee behaviours in cross-cultural assignments, concurrently an individual's own skills, abilities and other personality factors guide his/her behaviour in cross-cultural interaction. Together, these organizational and individual factors create certain tensions, which are accentuated by cultural differences and require further discussion.

Organizational Factors

Organizational factors in the current study affecting cross-cultural interaction comprise of organizational policies and norms. In the current sample, organizational policy dictated that most of the strategic decision-making positions were occupied by Chinese nationals in the energy, telecom and PSDP sectors. Since administrative roles were directed by Chinese management, organizational policies and norms were established according to Chinese guidelines. The lack of national diversity at the decision-making level created complex perceptions among Pakistani employees who were of the opinion that they were working under Chinese laws in an autocratic environment, lacking a voice in the decision-making processes. One Pakistani employee (E2P2) said:

> They have a dictator mindset; i.e. they follow single orders. They do not take time to discuss it. . . . As compared to the Pakistani way, we must take every-body on board and find a wise solution not like in a dictatorship.

The above response demonstrates that Pakistani employees prefer a democratic and collaborative decision-making process. However, for the sake of achieving targets and to reduce decision-making time, Chinese managers prefer autocratic decisions. The lack of a voice in decision-making has created dissatisfaction among Pakistani employees regarding Chinese managerial practices. In the long run, the problems such as lack of a voice in decision making, ignorance of different behavioural and cultural needs and lack of attention to high-potential employees can negatively affect the overall work environment (Brousseau et al., 2006).

The lack of overtime payments was another issue creating anxiety among Pakistani employees. For Chinese employees, the basic focus in CPEC projects was on-time completion of the projects. As a result, overtime work was considered normal for them and did not require compensation. One Chinese employee (PICI) reported:

> [I]n China we work beyond our job time. Sometimes we must work at night or during weekends.

Evidently, Chinese workplace culture and prevalent organizational policies over-looked overtime payments. However, Pakistani employees believed that overtime work was 'extra work' in relation to the stipulations of their contract; since they were sacrificing their family responsibilities for this extra work, they should be compensated. On the other hand, the Chinese administration considered this compensation an extra burden on company financial structures and believed work should be the 'ultimate objective' in the life of an employee. This difference in expectations created conflict among employees in the energy sector. One Pakistani employee (E2P2) grievingly said:

> They want to control us with Chinese laws. They don't believe in overtime payments. They should know Pakistani culture, its norms and policies applicable in Pakistan.

However, with evidence of Pakistani employees' performance being affected, the Chinese administration has realized the importance of flexibility in work schedules and overtime payments. The issue of overtime payments has been discussed in board meetings and has been under consideration by the Chinese administration to change the policy.

Reflection on organizational policies also revealed there were a wide range of employee training programmes, such as culture, pre-departure, orientation and language and skill-based training programmes. As discussed by previous literature, training is important for cross-cultural adjustment (see studies of Black & Gregersen, 1991; Rosenbusch et al., 2015) and is integral to employee efficiency. However, in the current sample, there were major sectoral differences in terms of training programmes provided to the employees. Background information from the sample studied revealed that all Chinese employees in PSDPs were given pre-departure and cultural training in China after joining the project (see Table 3.5 for basic characteristics). Similarly, in the energy sector, six months of cultural, pre-departure training and orientation was offered to employees. In contrast, most of the telecom sector employees had limited cultural and orientation training. The lack of formal orientation and pre-departure training forced employees to learn on the job by making mistakes and this frustrated both Chinese and Pakistani employees. Eventually, lack of basic training at the start of assignments and lack of effective cross-cultural communication norms alienated Chinese employees from Pakistani culture and hampered communication between the two nationalities.

Interviews with a number of managers revealed that deadlines of projects in the energy sector were largely affected by cross-cultural communication issues. The lack of a common language among employees – Chinese employees speaking Mandarin, and Pakistani employees speaking English and Urdu – has led the companies to prioritize language training. Similarly, certification courses in English and Mandarin were a mandatory requirement for PSDP employees. Cross-cultural language teaching projects in PSDPs focused on Mandarin and English proficiency for Pakistanis and Chinese employees, respectively. Moreover, before the assignment of Chinese employees to PSDPs in Pakistan, training in basic-level Urdu was provided by a number of Chinese universities. Similarly, orientation training in Chinese culture was mandatory in PSDPs for Pakistani employees.

Accordingly, Pakistani employees in the current sample working in PSDPs were proficient in Mandarin language and had fewer communication issues. In contrast, language training was totally absent in the telecom sector. This lack of training was the biggest challenge for Pakistani employees in their communication with the company's headquarters in China. Due to weak proficiency among Chinese employees in English and among Pakistani employees in Mandarin, employees in the companies' headquarters used translator services. However, the inefficiency persisted as technical terminology could not be easily translated into the other language. As mentioned by one Chinese employee (T2C3) in the telecom sector:

> I don't have an issue while communicating with headquarters but my Pakistani colleagues in the office request me to accompany them during live web chat with headquarters so that I can translate their views in Mandarin and speak to my colleagues in headquarters. Similarly, when they say something to the Pakistani team, I get the message across. It increases time but it's better than misunderstanding the critical points.

It is thus evident that Chinese employees provided language services to their Pakistani counterparts during critical board meetings and conversations. However, these translations and conversations cannot avert personal biases. See Table 3.5 for further comparisons across sectors.

On a positive note, skill-based training was provided in all sectors to employees, which was important for task clarity and job efficiency. The energy sector employees completed a six-month skill-based, off-the-job training in Chinese power plants. Similarly, PSDP employees experienced skill-based training in China and Pakistan. Telecom sector employees completed certification courses as part of their skill-based training for optimal achievement of project performance.

It can be observed from employee responses that of all the different types of training programmes across projects, language training was critical and essential for reducing miscommunication and increasing work efficiency. Thus, companies in both energy and PSDP sectors implemented company policies to improve the cross-cultural language proficiency of their employees. However, the telecom sector had no such policies which created frustration among employees.

Formal mentoring, as another organizational policy, was only practiced in the telecom sector, as observed in Table 3.5. The current sample of telecom sector companies offered a formal mentoring programme to their employees. A mentor was assigned to every new employee to acclimatize him/her to company policies, regulations and technical standard operating procedures. However, a formal mentoring programme was absent in the energy and PSDP sectors. In the energy sector, a few Pakistani employees (only 18 per cent) reported that they were assigned a Chinese mentor during their six months of training in China; later this mentor accompanied them to Pakistan. However, there was no policy in the energy sector for employee mentoring as such. Consequently, Pakistani employees in the energy sector pointed out their need for formal mentoring to enhance their technical skills and education regarding innate conversational patterns of Chinese culture which ultimately could help them understand Chinese supervisors' demands and expectations. Similar observations were recorded in the case of the PSDP sector where a formal mentoring programme was absent.

Besides organizational policies, certain organizational norms across sectors also modified and affected the behaviour of employees. Generally speaking, these norms guided the culturally established behaviours of employees, as well as constrained their actions in case of deviance from established norms. Intra-departmental and inter-departmental cooperation were strongly encouraged organizational norms across the sectors studied. Though cultural boundaries and preferences were evident in the energy and PSDP sectors, consultation preference was based on multiple factors. For example, if the project was unique, task complexity was high and confidential issues were involved, informal networks such as ex-colleagues, friends in different departments and ex-university fellows of the same nationality, were given preference. However, in the telecom sector, characterized by high professionalism, structured work and routine issues, team leaders or departmental heads were given autonomy in handling issues, irrespective of the managers' nationality.

Noticeably in all sectors, punctuality and time management were highly appraised organizational norms under the Chinese administration. In

Table 3.5 Organizational Characteristics Influencing Cross-Cultural Interactions

Energy Sector	Telecom Sector	PSDP Sector
Managerial positions filled mainly by Chinese; decision-making: Chinese management team; punctuality and time management were highly valued organizational norms under Chinese administration.	Managerial positions filled mainly by Chinese; decision-making: Chinese management team; punctuality and time management were highly valued organizational norms under Chinese administration.	Managerial positions filled mainly by Chinese; decision-making: Chinese management team; punctuality and time management were highly valued organizational norms under Chinese administration.
Six-month training programme: cross-cultural awareness and work-related orientation.	Limited cross-cultural awareness and work-related orientation training.	Pre-departure and cross-cultural awareness training in China.
Skill-based training for everyone. Mentoring programme is available.	Skill-based training for everyone. Formal mentoring programme is available.	Cross-cultural training is provided for locals. Skill-based training for everyone.
3:2 ratio of Pakistani to Chinese employees in the companies.	No language training programme.	No mentoring programme.
International experience: None. Only 1 employee had completed a 6-month cross-cultural student exchange programme.	3:2 ratio (approx.) of Pakistani to Chinese employees in the companies.	1:3 ratio of Pakistani to Chinese employees in the companies.
Socialization opportunities among Chinese and Pakistani employees were restricted to work sites where they had accommodation.	International experience: 23 per cent of the employees in the telecom sector had international experience. Most were Chinese.	International experience: All employees have international experience.
	Both nationalities could enjoy socializing outside the workplace.	Both nationalities could enjoy socializing outside the workplace.

monochromatic cultures (Shah, 2016), such as the Chinese culture, punctuality is extremely important and where meetings focus on 'one issue at one time', late arrival is considered highly unprofessional. Contrastingly, in polychromatic cultures (Shah, 2016), such as the Pakistani culture, time is considered flexible, deadlines are assumed to be flexible and interpersonal relationships have preference over time. As a result, Chinese employees complained about Pakistani employees wasting time in meeting and greeting their fellow colleagues (social interaction), taking lunch/prayer breaks and not arriving at official meetings on time. On the other hand, Pakistani employees reported that Chinese employees did not have families in Pakistan and lacked understanding of family commitments as well as other problems, such as transportation problems, which might jeopardize the commitment to punctuality. As one subject matter expert (SPM) reported:

> When I was working on the railroad project, I was being paid in dollars for the job. I was very excited and waited for my first salary. I knew before that the Chinese value time and that is why I tried to be on time for the job. However, when I received my first salary, it had certain deductions. When I asked my Chinese manager, he showed me a logbook which he maintained for the whole month (and which I didn't know about). The logbook had all the records about which day I used to come late, some days two minutes, another day four minutes etc. and cumulatively for the whole month, I was fifteen minutes late. I had no idea that he would not be flexible in the case of five-minute delays and would deduct my salary on this basis.

As shown, the different perceptions regarding time and punctuality were factors which affected the workplace atmosphere, and these also led to Chinese employees perceiving Pakistani employees as inefficient and irresponsible in terms of their duties.

Socialization in the workplace is another organizational norm which is essential for a healthy work environment and enables employees to integrate with their opposite culture in global assignments (Black & Gregersen, 1991). Although socialization opportunities varied across the sectors for both nationalities, socialization was an important element of formal and informal networking. The energy projects in Pakistan were site-based; these sites were located far from the cities and were considered critical factors influencing socialization. Hence, socialization activities of Chinese and Pakistani employees were restricted to the work site. The work site accommodation had basic facilities comprising grocery shops, gym, sport courts and kitchens/cafeterias for both nationalities. This arrangement facilitated socialization between employees from both nationalities after work, including at basketball matches, working out in the gym and celebrating birthdays and festivals. For the safety of international employees in Pakistan (i.e. Chinese employees in the CPEC projects), physical movement were restricted to certain cities. After long working hours, socialization for Chinese employees was mostly limited to their work site unless they obtained the necessary approval for off-site recreation from the Pakistani government. The lack of freedom to access off-site recreation and sight-seeing had increased loneliness and boredom among Chinese employees. In contrast, Pakistani employees could visit their homes on weekends in nearby cities and easily interacted with their Pakistani colleagues/friends in restaurants outside the work site. The telecom and PSDP projects were relatively unrestricted in nature and were located in Islamabad, the capital city where the security situation was generally good. Therefore, both nationality employees could enjoy socializing in restaurants, hiking and inviting others to their homes for dinner on special occasions. Overall, the organizational factors identified earlier highlighted the integral contributing and inhibiting factors to employee adjustment. These findings address the question of the way in which organizations enable individuals to engage in cross-cultural interaction. Nevertheless, individual factors also contribute to employee adjustment/maladjustment and require further investigation.

Individual Factors

An employee's personal profile and his/her personality characteristics also require adjustment in a new cross-cultural assignment. When an individual joins an assignment and is faced with contrasting demands, his/her attitude towards the different demands along with personal characteristics also affects his/her work performance. The family situation was one of the factors that affected performance among both Chinese and Pakistani employees. For example, most Chinese employees in the energy and telecom sectors had moved to Pakistan without their families. A number of reasons accounted for the lack of family accompaniment, including the short-term nature of the work, security and schooling. Consequently, most Chinese employees felt lonely and indulged deeply in work. The sense of urgency was evident during the interviews in the employees' eagerness to complete assignments and return to China as early as possible. A typical Chinese employee in the CPEC projects worked 14–15 hours per day, with an afternoon nap in the office along with lunch, coffee and toilet breaks (based on responses from Chinese employees). In the energy sector, company policy stipulated that Chinese employees could travel to China to visit their families every three months. Nevertheless, these employees felt nostalgic while talking about their families during the interviews, as visits back home during assignments were considered short and employees wanted to spend more time in China with their families. On the other hand, Pakistani employees were living with their families and had full family responsibility. According to Pakistani norms, an employee will spend 8–9 hours on average per day at work as well as take lunch and toilet breaks. There is no culture of a midday nap during working hours in Pakistan (based on the researcher's own background within Pakistani society). The differences in family situation and work norms between host and home country employees created tensions among employees. Adherence to deadlines and completion of work targets acted as motivators for the Chinese. However, Pakistani employees aspired to complete daily targets in normal working hours and then go home to their families for the remaining part of the day. Overtime work was highly disliked by Pakistani employees. In order to avoid overtime work payments and conflicting demands between family and work, flexible working hours were considered by a few supervisors. In explaining the change of work tactics, a Chinese employee in a supervisory role (T1C4) said:

> At first, I pushed them (Pakistani employees) to do late shifts and complete the work. However, then I observed that my employee efficiency was decreasing every day. Then I said to my employees, you should go home by 6 pm and it's okay if you can send me a report by 11 pm at night. In this way, he was present in his home, and spending time with his family after office hours but at the same time working remotely on the task assigned. As a result, he was flexible and efficient in meeting the deadlines.

Hence, since tension between family commitments and work was a burden for the Pakistani employees, instead of following the over-time work policy for both nationalities, Chinese supervisors adopted a flexi-time policy for Pakistani employees. This solution enabled Pakistani employees to give time to their families as well as to work.

Another factor affecting cross-cultural employee adjustment was the previous international experience of individual employees and their work exposure to multicultural assignments. Employees' previous international experience enables individuals to embrace the diversity of cultural issues through their openness to experiences while maintaining the geocentric orientation of international assignments (Taylor et al., 2008). Gradually, employees can build their capability to manage cultural differences effectively in the workplace. Among the interview respondents, all employees in the PSDP sector had diverse international experience before joining the CPEC projects in Pakistan. However, none of the sample employees in the energy sector had previous international work experience, and only 2 Chinese and 1 Pakistani employee out of 13 sample employees in the telecom sector had previous international experience (See Table 3.2). This lack of international experience of home country employees was the major contributing factor to employee maladjustment and dissatisfaction in the telecom and energy sectors where it was found that Chinese employees lacked flexibility and understanding of diverse cultural norms. Similarly, Pakistani employees faced difficulty in understanding their Chinese counterparts' working style, behaviours, cultural norms and communication patterns due to a lack of previous international experience. Nevertheless, PSDP employees from both sides were more satisfied and were able to adjust to their assignments due to English language proficiency, along with previous international experience that enhanced the adjustment to a new cultural environment.

The aforementioned discussion has led to another key finding of this study regarding the importance of employee cross-cultural language proficiency. Language proficiency and language compatibility across cultures improve communication satisfaction (Downs & Hazen, 1977) among employees. Although English is not the first language of either nationality, English is the basic means of communication in Pakistan in schools, universities and official settings since the country was under British rule for many years (1858–1947). English is the official language for written communication in the private and public sectors in Pakistan and written and spoken English is imparted from the initial years of schooling in most schools. Moreover, a candidate's response in English during a job or promotion interview is considered one of the criteria of good communication skills. This language proficiency was also evident in our interviews as Pakistani employees' English competency in the sample was relatively good. The interviews showed that Pakistani employees in the telecom and energy sectors lacked knowledge of Mandarin and Chinese employees in the headquarters of the telecom and energy sectors lacked English proficiency, thus communication problems existed for both nationalities. Most Chinese employees had learnt written English skills in high school for the purpose of passing their examinations, but not oral English communication skills. One of the Chinese employees (TIC3) commented:

> [I]n China we only learn English in school, in a university or only in middle school. That is, we study only for the exam but not for speaking. Even in the class, we learn basic words like ok . . . this is an egg, this laptop. So mostly we speak Chinese. That is why Chinese English is not very good.

In the energy sector in particular, most of the Chinese employees had a vocabulary of very few English words and lacked clarity of expression. Due to the lack of a common language and poor English pronunciation of Chinese employees, language barriers and communication issues arose between the two nationalities. One Chinese employee (E2C1) identified the challenges in cross-cultural communication as follows:

> Pakistanis didn't have a thermal power plant before. So, this work is new for a Pakistani engineer and Chinese engineers have to teach (train) Pakistani engineers; but because Chinese engineers cannot speak English, our training work is very hard. Our Pakistani engineers always complain that they cannot learn how to operate the power plant because Chinese engineers cannot teach them. So, this is the biggest problem at the moment.

Thus, due to a lack of cross-language understanding between the two nationalities as well as the weak proficiency in English of the Chinese employees, the level of communication satisfaction among energy sector employees was very low. Chinese employees in the telecom sector had relatively better English proficiency than employees in the energy sector, but Pakistani employees had difficulty in understanding their Chinese counterparts' communication patterns and accents. However, the issue was somewhat less serious in the telecom sector compared to the energy sector. One reason was the similarity of technical language and standard operating procedures between the telecom sectors of China and Pakistan, which made communication relatively easier. Yet, most of the Chinese employees in the telecom sector still considered communication and language proficiency to be the biggest barrier in managing the project efficiently.

Among the individual factors in the current sample, it was observed that an individual's own cross-cultural capability, including proactiveness, self-awareness, socialization initiative, networking and openness to experience, was the biggest factor to escalate or diminish the issues of cross-cultural adjustment. Generally speaking, employees who are more extrovert, open to experience, actively participate in networking, take risks and have a high level of self-awareness, face fewer difficulties in adjusting to cross-cultural assignments. In contrast, if employees are introvert, they are generally inhibited, have high uncertainty avoidance and tend to be reactive when responding to issues, instead of proactively engaging and developing strategies to mitigate those problems. Consequently, employees hiding in cocoons during their cross-cultural assignment would have more difficulties in adjusting in comparison to employees who are open to the new environment and willing to adjust.

Cross-Cultural Adjustment and Outcomes

In addition to the direct effects of existing cultural norms in both nationalities, individual and organizational factors act as interactional facets for adjustment/maladjustment. Maladjustment in cross-cultural assignments may result in poor performance and frustration (Wu & Ang, 2011), and that could be attributable to organizational and individual factors (e.g. technical knowledge and relationships with host and home country employees). These difficulties, together with inhibiting factors, could jeopardize the optimal project performance goals and may result in project failure. As a result of employees' cross-cultural differences and the associated problems, both Chinese and Pakistani employees were required to make certain adjustments. Skills enhancement and personality modifications by both nationalities could be integral to overcoming these problems.

Employee Adjustment

Interview findings revealed that Chinese and Pakistani employees made certain adjustments along the process of project development compared to the lack of adjustment at the beginning of their assignment. Employees identified several areas as important for making an adjustment, including changing work attitude, improving skills for adopting new techniques, improving cooperation, enhancing language capability, building networks and developing effective communication between home and host country employees. However, there are certain adjustments which are beyond employees' self-initiative capabilities and require collegial (peers and supervisors) and organizational support, as discussed in the following section.

Employee Initiative

At the beginning of assignments, employees faced multiple adjustment issues and frustrations. However, over time employees realized that adjustment was imperative and required learning from their mistakes. Employee adjustment was equally important for host as well as home country employees. Many Chinese employees reported that they became more flexible, polite and appreciated Pakistani employees' cultural values after observing local cultural norms and made adjustment accordingly. Similarly, during their interaction with their Chinese counterparts, Pakistani employees learnt new technology, skills, techniques and working styles. For example, one of the Pakistani employees (TIP3) described his adjustment to the Chinese work culture:

> I have found over my four years of work in this project, that my company requires hard work and commitment from employees. Chinese culture and company will support only those employees who can work day and night. . . . The main thing is attitude, if your attitude is that of a workaholic and you are eager to learn, it is the only way that you can survive in Chinese companies.

As shown earlier, Pakistani employees were inspired by Chinese employees' working attitudes and adjusted by adopting the characteristics of punctuality, hard work and time management. As a proactive gesture to promote socialization, Chinese employees in the telecom sector have started learning basic Urdu. Moreover, Chinese employees initiated personal and professional relationships with their Pakistani counterparts in order to improve their networking skills. However, smooth network entry appeared to be a challenging goal due to communication misunderstandings, language barriers and lack of networking knowledge in relation to Pakistani cultural norms. Moreover, the power distance instilled in Pakistani culture, inhibited Pakistani employees in overcoming psychological barriers to developing friendships with Chinese managers.

A significant increase in socialization activities by Pakistani employees with Chinese counterparts was evident after adjustment. Due to improved security conditions and relatively quick government approvals in Pakistan after 2017, Pakistani and Chinese employees could commute and socialize relatively easily in public places and at local festivals. Although Chinese employees preferred other Chinese employees for socialization and networking (due to the ease of communication), festivities of both nationalities were celebrated together. As a gesture of respect and harmony, Pakistani employees participated in the mid-autumn festival and Chinese New Year with their Chinese colleagues. Pakistani employees' fondness of Chinese cuisines and interaction in festivals also enhanced the relationship building between both nationalities. This shared experience developed a broader vision of Chinese culture by Pakistani employees and reduced communication barriers. Chinese employees developed comradeship with Pakistani employees, who in turn considered Chinese employees as their friends. Clearly, there were positive outcomes for both sides. As one Pakistani employee (E2P1) said:

> We all are settling quite well now . . . because you know, Pakistanis are my brothers, Chinese are my friends.

Collegial Support

Collegial support was another factor that smoothed employee adjustment in CPEC projects. The level of cooperation increased after adjustments were made by both host and home country employees, with improvement of cross-cultural understanding and trustworthy relationships. As one Chinese employee (E2C3) said about his Pakistani colleague:

> He knows more things and he can do some work which I can't do; for example, he can go to the market and buy some things for me at a low price and he can bargain.

The statement reveals that the level of trust and friendship increased among both nationalities through adequate adjustment. Most Chinese employees became accustomed to Pakistani norms after the first year of their assignment in Pakistan. It was reported by Pakistani employees that, although Chinese supervisors were strict at the beginning of an assignment about late shifts, the supervisors later became more flexible regarding the time arrangement. For example, in the telecom sector, Chinese supervisors permitted Pakistani employees to observe standard official working hours and complete the remaining work at home. Consequently, this enabled employees to achieve the required outcome as well as maintain a work-family balance. Furthermore, Chinese supervisors in the telecom sector became more considerate towards the religious responsibilities of Pakistani employees by allowing them to have prayer breaks during working hours. However, prayer breaks were still not allowed in the energy sectors due to the critical nature of the work.

Organizational Support

Organizational efforts were found crucial for effective employee adjustment. For example, in order to address the availability of Chinese food, companies in the telecom sector separated the Chinese kitchen from the general one. In the Chinese kitchen, food was cooked by Chinese chefs with licensed Chinese ingredients and other materials. However, Chinese employees in the PSDP sector lacked such facilities and yearned for Chinese cuisines in Pakistan. Despite the separate cafés at the worksite for both nationalities in the energy sector, pork and liquor were still prohibited in these cafés in accordance with Pakistani laws. Chinese employees were encouraged to become familiar with Pakistani cuisines by experiencing the local dinner parties. As one Chinese employee explained when sharing his adjustment process:

> I have acquired several skills and now like to stay here in Pakistan. For instance, I can drive easily here in Pakistan; in China driving is very difficult and strict. Also, I have adopted some eating habits like eating beef, mutton and some *samosa*, *karahi* and *chapati* (flat bread). Initially I tried

the Pakistani food at official dinners and I really liked it. So, I enjoy Pakistani food now and when I go to China, this food is not available there and I sometimes miss it.

With regard to the question of how organizations enable individuals engaging in cross-cultural interaction to be effective and to achieve positive outcomes, organizational support has played a vital role in employee interactions. Local dinner parties and festivity celebrations were used to facilitate cross-cultural understanding and cross-cultural bonding. As the next step to acculturation, Chinese employees were also encouraged to attend the celebration of Pakistani festivals such as Eid and Ramadan, with their Pakistani colleagues. In addition, the PSDP sector initiated cross-cultural awareness programmes, such as food carnivals, social events and workshops, as part of a cross-cultural awareness campaign. One Chinese employee (PIC2) explained:

> Next week we are going to hold the mid-autumn festival and also celebrate our national day. On that day different teachers have different tasks to perform, like my task is to make Chinese Tea. This is to show our Chinese tea culture, to introduce our tea to Pakistan and then to have cross-cultural communication and interaction with stall displays; to let Pakistanis find out more things about our culture.

As language training is a precursor to communication satisfaction, Chinese employees have started to learn the English language and basic Urdu through training programmes initiated by their companies. For example, after the commencement of the construction phase, energy companies made language training mandatory for every employee as part of company policy. As a result, every week all Chinese employees attended three-hour English and Urdu classes. In addition, language training courses were also considered essential for Pakistani employees in the energy sector who attended a three-hour weekend class of Mandarin every week. Pakistani employees realized that, by learning Mandarin, they could develop a friendship with Chinese employees as well as promote harmony and collaboration between the two sides. As one Pakistani employee (E2P3) said: "If you say something in the mother tongue of another person, it will enter his heart. So, I am learning Mandarin so that I can enter their heart."

However, language courses were still absent in the telecom sector and employees expressed the need for these courses. In general, employee adjustment is a two-way process which requires mutual collaboration and support through strong social networks and networking initiatives. Eventually, social networks and employee adjustment contribute to a favourable work environment for creativity, innovation and efficiency. Cross-cultural understanding and adequate employee adjustment were the results of Chinese and Pakistani employees' mutually supportive attitudes. Nevertheless, many behavioural and attitudinal adjustments were required at an individual level for both nationalities. On the other hand, some forms of stress, anxiety and confusion can be seen as motivating factors for making an adjustment and learning about another country's culture in order to build a workable relationship (Rosenbusch et al., 2015).

Project Objectives

In order to quantify the impact of employee adjustment and social networking on the achievement of project outcomes in Stage Two of the study, the current qualitative findings have helped in identifying project objectives which measure the CPEC projects performance across sectors. These project outcomes are further analysed in quantitative research to measure their relationship with the concerned variables. Moreover, the identified project objectives helped to answer another research question, namely, how organizations enable individuals engaging in cross-cultural interaction to be effective and to achieve positive outcomes. The project objectives identified in the qualitative phase helped in measuring the influence of social networks and networking behaviour on these objectives in the quantitative phase. Optimal project performance in the CPEC is the essential requirement of the Chinese and Pakistani governments. However, effective employee adjustment is a fundamental factor for optimal project performance goals in the case of international assignments, as maladjusted employees hamper work efficiency and delay project objectives. For example, in this study, organizational support, including language training programmes and healthy work environment, discipline, interdepartmental cooperation and socialization opportunities, was helpful in employee adjustment and ultimately optimal project performance goals. Similarly, employee initiatives, such as proactiveness and socialization along with collegial support, paved the path towards employee adjustment and optimal project performance goals. Moreover, findings generated a notable variation of project objectives and deliverables across the sectors due to differences in projects. For example, major project objectives in the energy sector were electricity shortage mitigation, early completion of the project, fewer employee conflicts, cross-cultural harmony, reduction in cost and wastage, reduction in communication misunderstandings and language barriers. Most importantly, mitigation of electricity shortage was the basic objective across all projects along with timely delivery of power plants to the Pakistani government.

In the PSDP sector, the project objectives were to achieve successful completion of the CPEC projects as well as social reforms. In this regard, as a part of social reforms, cultural exchange programme for students was also initiated by Pakistani universities working together with Chinese language training institutes. As part of PSDP training programme, the Chinese language training institutes obtained funding from the Chinese government and provided scholarships for students to learn Chinese language. The total number of students dramatically increased after the initiation of CPEC in 2015, such as the total number of applicants in 2014 was 400; 2015 was 671; 2016 was 1350; and 2017 was 3,650 (reported by P1C1). The future of Chinese language training programme is based upon the success of the CPEC projects with employment opportunities being created to hire these students with Chinese language proficient.

Lastly, the project objectives in the telecom sector were varied and included responsiveness to client needs, successful product development, maintenance of optical fibre, application development, departmental support, reduction in costs and wastage, increase in speed of product to market, quality improvement and, most importantly, the clear alignment of project goals to strategic goals and vision of company.

As observed, the identified project objectives and deliverables define the breadth and depth of the CPEC objectives to be accomplished by companies working on these projects. However, in all sectors, reduction in costs, time management and quality management were observed to be the required project performance goals. All other objectives supported these three basic performance attributes (project objectives) of the projects. The exploration of these project objectives aided in measuring project performance goals in the subsequent quantitative study. The meta-analytical study of Ahmed et al. (2019) suggests that "project completion delays are one of the most realistic problems that the Pakistani and Chinese administration faces to achieve its true potential" (p. 6). Hence, the timely achievement of project objectives while maintaining a mandate is important and is possible only if effective employee adjustments occur accordingly.

3.5 Discussion of Interview Findings

The current qualitative study has explored the phenomenon of social networking approaches across different cultures and has identified the project objectives of the CPEC projects. Furthermore, the influence of national cultures has been explored in the 'two-way adjustment' of cross-cultural employees in the CPEC. This study has explored different cultural norms, organizational and individual factors. The research findings clearly suggest that cultural elements have a direct impact on the behaviour and productivity of employees working on the CPEC projects. The findings reveal that Chinese and Pakistani employee behaviours share similarities but also indicate differences. It is also evident that there are idiosyncratic social networking processes among both Chinese and Pakistani employees, and these directly affect cross-cultural adjustment and eventual outcomes. The cultural and perceptual differences between both nationalities require strategies to address the maladjustment issues, as discussed in Section 3.4.

As stated by Marx (2011), home country employees face challenges, and their anxieties vary from mild to the extreme, depending on the level of cultural similarity/diversity compared to their home country. Accordingly, home country employees' major challenges include: the strain of effort to adapt to a new culture, the sense of loss as well as feelings of deprivation (friends, status, family and possessions), feelings of rejection by members of the host culture, confusion with regard to values, identity and role, anxiety and anger about 'foreign' practices and feelings of hopelessness in the struggle with the new environment. As home country employees, Chinese employees faced anxiety in the new cultural environment, confusion in the religious value system of the host country and feelings of deprivation due to being alone while on assignment. However, perceptual differences regarding Chinese work practices also affected Pakistani employees, the host country employees, which was caused by the lack of supervisor support (from the Chinese) in certain cases. This resulted in feelings of alienation by Pakistani employees in their own country and maladjustment in the cross-cultural work environment.

The multifaceted work challenges and attitudinal differences as a result of Chinese and Pakistani employees' interactions were accompanied by communication problems, differences in understanding of religious activities and differences of networking behaviour. These cultural interactions led to certain organizational and individual problems which affected cross-cultural employee adjustment. Across the sectors, organizational-level problems regarding policies and norms influenced the supervisory as well as team-level employees. These organizational problems included lack of flexibility in working hours (of Pakistani employees), lack of language training within organizations (especially in the telecom sector) and differences in socialization opportunities for Chinese and Pakistani employees. Eventually, the effects of these cultural and organizational problems trickled down to the individual level. The trickling effect created a further challenge for an individual to adjust into the new environment, especially where an individual lacked cross-cultural competency, that is, a set of congruent behaviours and attitudes that come together in a system to work effectively in cross-cultural situations (Konanahalli et al., 2014). These challenges required individual, collegial and organizational initiatives for better employee adjustment in order to achieve the overall objectives.

Fundamentally, the Chinese employees had a task-oriented vision of the CPEC projects, and their workaholic and disciplined work nature marked them as high achievers. Whereas Pakistani employees believed in a work-family balance, strong personal *hawalas* (personal connection), had a distinct time frame for daily tasks and believed in life after work. This behaviour created perceptual differences whereby Chinese employees considered Pakistani employees to be careless and negligent of deadlines. In contrast, Pakistani employees considered Chinese supervisors to be workaholic and indifferent towards family responsibilities. Clearly, the variance of work preferences and flexi-time arrangements should be realized by the supervisors in managing their employees for better operations in the future work.

Further insights into individuals' work profiles reveal that in addition to the lack of family presence for the Chinese employees, weak cross-language proficiency between the nationalities resulted in employee maladjustment. Lack of international experience of both nationalities and employees' passive attitude towards networking further contributed to maladjustment.

Previous research conducted within a single nationality homogeneous network of Chinese employees shows that there is an overlap between work and social interaction among Chinese employees (Bu & Roy, 2005). In China, building *guanxi* requires extra effort to be involved in the personal and social lives of others (e.g. social exchanges and recreational events) as well as allowing others to be involved in the individual's own non-work life (Bu & Roy, 2005). However, even in cross-cultural projects such as the CPEC, Chinese employees developed *guanxi* between their own nationality employees and interacted to a greater extent among themselves socially as well as professionally; they did not make a dedicated effort to accept Pakistani nationals (heterophily) into their network. The same nationality in-group preferences (homophily) prevalent among the project members inhibited their exposure to views of other nationality employees. In contrast to the study of Bu and Roy (2005), in our cross-cultural research, Chinese employees were mindful of their professional and personal *guanxi* (distinct social ties) and dealt with Pakistani employees as outgroup members. These distinct social ties with cross-cultural employees indicate Chinese employees' preference to interact with their own nationality and lack of willingness to embrace local networking norms and heterophilic ties. This situation further reinforces the psychological barrier of the supervisor-subordinate relationship (where the Chinese are supervisors and Pakistanis are subordinates) between the two nationalities.

It is contended that the Chinese are motivated to develop overlapping professional and personal ties among their own nationals in homogeneous as well as in cross-cultural collaborative projects. However, in cross-cultural projects, homophilic ties create seclusion from other nationalities, inbred information and lack of understanding of workplace and social norms of other cultures, eventually resulting in anxiety and maladjustment in cross-cultural projects. On the other hand, Pakistani employees initiated efforts to develop networks with their Chinese counterparts. Pakistani employees utilized professional and personal *hawalas* interchangeably in their personal and professional life, which was perceived as a lack of professionalism by Chinese employees. Moreover, according to the Pakistani employees, language barriers and lack of knowledge of networking norms of the Chinese were the biggest barriers to heterophilic network development.

The lack of understanding of cross-nationality work-related views due to homophily, language barriers, incompatibility of religious beliefs, lack of family support, and social and living condition differences, creates misunderstandings. Though the studies of Rosenbusch et al. (2015), Young (2013), Konanahalli et al. (2014) and Carraher et al. (2004) highlighted similar issues for home country employee adjustment, this study reveals that cross-cultural networking, strong supportive social networks and the resulting cross-cultural adjustment are equally important for both host and home country employees. Pakistani employees require more diligent work practices, including punctuality and hard work, to cope with the demands of Chinese supervisors. Regardless of nationality, culturally smart/competent (Chen, 2019) individuals can efficiently achieve cross-cultural adjustment and project goals. These individuals can manage the cultural differences by means of the adaptive strategies of enrolling in training programmes, obtaining mentoring opportunities, developing socializing strategies and networking through different activities. Dedicated efforts at organizational level are thus also required to develop cultural diversity in supervisory positions, standardized training programmes for cross-language proficiency, formal mentoring programmes and networking avenues such as excursions and cultural festivals for cross-cultural adjustment.

Furthermore, cross-cultural adjustment is not only an individual effort, but a collective effort at the individual and collegial levels. At the collegial level, the required adjustment involves building mutual understanding among group members, engaging group decision making and achieving common goals. Therefore, it is important for employees to understand the adequate level of adjustment, which includes work-related and general living adjustments. A two-way ongoing adjustment is required for both host and home country employees in cross-cultural working environment, based on the priorities of these employees. For example, for the Chinese, the priority could be interactional adjustment with host country employees to overcome loneliness and develop mutual understanding. For Pakistanis, the priority could be work-related adjustment such as punctuality and hard work in order to achieve the overall objectives.

In addition, the nature of a problem (simple versus complex, structured versus unstructured), context (i.e. early or late project phase; or employee tenure in a company) and time spent on a project will determine the level of effort and networking required in a situation. A complex issue in an unstructured situation will certainly require an extra networking effort by an employee to overcome uncertainty because of the early phase of a project and less time spent in certain projects (e.g. energy sector).

Networking and employee adjustment is a laborious process which requires patience and time to give beneficial results in cross-cultural assignments. In this regard, this study has elucidated supportive factors and adjustment challenges.

3.6 Summary

This chapter offered detailed insights into interview findings conducted with Chinese and Pakistani employees in the CPEC projects across three sectors. The major finding is that employee adjustment is a complex process which requires attention to detail and where the role of networking is integral to achieve positive outcomes. The issues are related to three major themes, namely, cultural differences, organizational factors and individual factors, and these influence cross-cultural employee adjustment and project outcomes. As observed, employee socialization, networking norms, cross-cultural language proficiency, cross-cultural networks and previous international experience are important elements enhancing effective employee adjustment.

Additionally, the current chapter provides evidence for further study on the role of social networks as well as networking behaviour influencing cross-cultural employee adjustment along with other variables of interest by means of a quantitative study. In light of identified factors and understanding of in-depth cultural interaction, the effects of these factors are studied in detail in the quantitative phase. Therefore, the next chapter focuses on the quantitative analysis (i.e. Stage Two of the study) and will tackle questions regarding the relationships between social networks, networking behaviour and employee adjustment along with communication satisfaction, conflict management and project performance.

References

Adler, E. S., & Clark, R. (2014). *An invitation to social research: How it's done* (5th ed.). Stamford, CT: Cengage Learning.
Ahmed, S., Ali, A., Kumar, D., Malik, M. Z., & Memon, A. H. (2019). China Pakistan economic corridor and Pakistan's energy security: A meta-analytic review. *Energy Policy*, *127*, 147–154.
Albert, E. (2018). *The state of religion in China*. Retrieved 16 April 2019, from www.cfr.org/backgrounder/religion-china
Bansal, P., & Corley, K. (2011). The coming of age for qualitative research: Embracing the diversity of qualitative methods. *Academy of Management Journal*, *54*, 233–237.
Baumann, C., Hamin, H., & Yang, S. J. (2016). Work ethic formed by pedagogical approach: Evolution of institutional approach to education and competitiveness. *Asia Pacific Business Review*, *22*(3), 374–396.
Black, J. S., & Gregersen, H. B. (1991). Antecedents to cross-cultural adjustment for expatriates in Pacific rim assignments. *Human Relations*, *44*, 497–515.
Braun, V., & Clarke, V. (2006). Using thematic analysis in psychology. *Qualitative Research in Psychology*, *3*(2), 77–101.
Brinkmann, S. (2014). Doing without data. *Qualitative Inquiry*, *20*(6), 720–725.
Brousseau, K. R., Driver, M. J., Hourihan, G., & Larsson, R. (2006). The seasoned executive's decision-making style. *Harvard Business Review*, *84*(2), 110–121.
Bu, N., & Roy, J. P. (2005). Career success networks in China: Sex differences in network composition and social exchange practices. *Asia Pacific Journal of Management*, *22*(4), 381–403.
Burki, S. J., & Ziring, L. (2019). *Pakistan*. Encyclopedia Britannica, Inc. Retrieved 16 April 2019, from www.britannica.com/place/Pakistan
Carraher, S. M., Scott, C., & Carraher, S. C. (2004). A comparison of polychronicity levels among small business owners and non-business owners in the US, China, Ukraine, Poland, Hungary, Bulgaria, and Mexico. *International Journal of Family Business*, *1*(1), 97–101.
Cassell, C. M. (2015). *Interviewing for business and management students*. London: Sage.
Chen, M. (2019). The impact of expatriates' cross-cultural adjustment on work stress and job involvement in the high-tech industry. *Frontiers in Psychology*, *10*, 2228.
Chiu, R. K., & Kosinski Jr, F. A. (1995). Chinese cultural collectivism and work-related stress: Implications for employment counselors. *Journal of Employment Counselling*, *32*(3), 98–110.
Dikko, M. (2016). Establishing construct validity and reliability: Pilot testing of a qualitative interview for research in takaful (Islamic insurance). *The Qualitative Report*, *21*(3), 521–528.
Downs, C. W., & Hazen, M. D. (1977). A factor analytic study of communication satisfaction. *The Journal of Business Communication*, *14*(3), 63–73.
Edhlund, B., & McDougall, A. (2019). *NVivo 12 essentials*. Retrieved 18 January 2021, from Lulu.com.
Eisenhardt, K. M. (1989). Making fast strategic decisions in high-velocity environments. *Academy of Management Journal*, *32*(3), 543–576.
Gioia, D. A., & Chittipeddi, K. (1991). Sensemaking and sense giving in strategic change initiation. *Strategic Management Journal*, *12*, 433–448.

Gioia, D. A., Corley, K. G., & Hamilton, A. L. (2013). Seeking qualitative rigor in inductive research: Notes on the Gioia methodology. *Organizational Research Methods, 16*(1), 15–31.

Haider, M. (2014). *Alcohol consumption in Pakistan: Don't mix sin with crime.* Retrieved 26 September 2019, from www.dawn.com/news/1141153

Hall, E. T., & Hall, M. R. (1989). *Understanding cultural differences.* Yarmouth, ME: Intercultural press.

Kim, Y. (2011). The pilot study in qualitative inquiry: Identifying issues and learning lessons for culturally competent research. *Qualitative Social Work, 10*(2), 190–206.

King, N. (2004). Using templates in the thematic analysis of text. In C. Cassell & G. Symon (Eds.), *Essential guide to qualitative methods in organizational research* (pp. 256–270). London: Sage.

Konanahalli, A., Oyedele, L. O., Spillane, J., Coates, R., von Meding, J., & Ebohon, J. (2014). Cross-cultural intelligence (CQ): Its impact on British expatriate adjustment on international construction projects. *International Journal of Managing Projects in Business, 7*(3), 423–448.

Luborsky, M. R., & Rubinstein, R. L. (1995). Sampling in qualitative research: Rationale, issues and methods. *Research on Aging, 17,* 89–113.

Marx, E. (2011). *Breaking through culture shock: What you need to succeed in international business.* London: Nicholas Brealey Publishing.

Mason, J. (2002). *Qualitative researching* (2nd ed.). London: Sage.

Miles, M. B., & Huberman, A. M. (2014). *Qualitative data analysis, a methods sourcebook* (3rd ed.). Thousand Oaks, CA: Sage.

Nadeem, S., & Kayani, N. (2019). Sifarish: Understanding the ethical versus unethical use of network-based hiring in Pakistan. *Journal of Business Ethics, 158*(4), 969–982.

Nazarian, A., Atkinson, P., & Foroudi, P. (2017). Influence of national culture and balanced organizational culture on the hotel industry's performance. *International Journal of Hospitality Management, 63,* 22–32.

Patton, M. Q. (1990). *Qualitative evaluation and research methods* (2nd ed.). Newbury Park, CA: Sage.

The Pew Forum on Religion & Public Life. (2012). *The world's Muslims: Unity and diversity.* Washington: Pew Research Centre.

Robinson, O. (2014). Sampling in interview-based qualitative research: A theoretical and practical guide. *Qualitative Research in Psychology, 11,* 25–41.

Rosenbusch, K., Cerny, L. J., & Earnest, D. R. (2015). The impact of stressors during international assignments. *Cross Cultural Management: An International Journal, 22*(3), 405–430.

Saldaña, J. (2015). *The coding manual for qualitative researchers.* Thousand Oaks, CA: Sage.

Shah, S. (2016). Cross-cultural view of rape. *Southern California Review of Law & Social Justice, 26*(2), 75–101.

Sousa, D. (2014). Validation in qualitative research: General aspects and specificities of the descriptive phenomenological method. *Qualitative Research in Psychology, 11*(2), 211–227.

Strauss, A., & Corbin, J. (1990). *Basics of qualitative research.* Newbury Park, CA: Sage.

Taylor, S., Levy, O., Boyacigiller, N. A., & Beechler, S. (2008). Employee commitment in MNCs: Impacts of organizational culture, HRM and top management orientations. *The International Journal of Human Resource Management*, *19*(4), 501–527.

Wu, P. C., & Ang, S. H. (2011). The impact of expatriate supporting practices and cultural intelligence on cross-cultural adjustment and performance of expatriates in Singapore. *The International Journal of Human Resource Management*, *22*(13), 2683–2702.

Yang, K., & Banamah, A. (2014). Quota sampling as an alternative to probability sampling? An experimental study. *Sociological Research Online*, *19*(1), 1–11.

Yin, R. K. (2009). *Case study research: Design and methods*. Beverly Hills, CA: Sage.

Young, B. (2013). Managing projects in China – what could possibly go wrong? Article 4 – Dragons, Camels and Kangaroos. *PM World Journal*, *2*(6), 1–7.

4 Survey Results

4.1 Introduction

The previous chapter presented and discussed data from the semi-structured interviews and the associated critical findings. The Chinese and Pakistani employees revealed their insights regarding social network development and networking behaviour, cross-cultural adjustment challenges and overall project outcomes across three sectors. Evidence gathered in Stage One indicated that employee cross-cultural language proficiency, socialization, networking norms, cross-cultural networks and previous international experience of employees are key factors for effective employee adjustment and achieving project goals. In this chapter, we present the quantitative study aimed at addressing questions regarding the relationships between social networks, networking behaviour and employee adjustment along with communication satisfaction, conflict management and project performance.

Section 4.2 explains the survey development based on interview findings and provides the rationale for formulating a number of hypotheses. Section 4.3 presents the data collection procedure and explains the data screening and analysis technique. Moreover, this section discusses the equivalence and factor analysis in cross-cultural studies, followed by a descriptive analysis of the Chinese and Pakistani samples, as well as the mean comparison of networking behaviour and employee adjustment between Chinese and Pakistani employees. Section 4.4 presents the results based on correlation analysis for independent and dependent variables of the Chinese and Pakistani samples, along with hierarchical regression and moderation analysis. In conclusion, a summary is presented in section 4.5.

4.2 Survey Development

As Stage Two of this study, the quantitative survey emphasized the applicability of the study of the relationship between social networks and networking behaviour in perceived employee adjustment among Chinese and Pakistani employees. The survey also focused on employee adjustment enhancing the realization of project performance goals, conflict management and communication satisfaction.

Two sets of similar surveys were designed for Chinese and Pakistani employees working at the managerial level. Initially, both surveys were developed in English. The surveys were pre-tested and pilot-tested for accuracy, reduction

DOI: 10.4324/9781003240815-4

of respondent burden and order of questions. The surveys were also tested for response latency, that is, the time taken to complete individual items as well as the full survey (Lavrakas, 2008). The pre-testing was performed by an expert in the field of quantitative research and linguistic changes were suggested to clarify certain survey items. The suggested changes were incorporated into the survey and pilot testing was undertaken with five respondents from each nationality working in the CPEC projects.

Survey Instrument

The survey instrument for Chinese and Pakistani nationals was developed after an extensive literature review. The survey provided for multiple scale items for each of the variables in the hypothesized model. The measures and scales used in this study were drawn from previous studies to ensure reliability and validity. All the utilized scales had a reliability and internal consistency greater than 0.70 (Nunnally, 1978) and were adapted from previous studies (i.e. the scale values are adopted directly from studies of (Bader & Schuster, 2015; Burt, 1992; Wang & Nayir, 2006). The positive to negative worded scale values, such as 4=very close, 1=not very close, 1= very much adjusted and 5=very unadjusted/very uncomfortable, are adopted from previous studies. Identical set of survey items was utilized for both nationalities, except for cross-cultural employee adjustment. The cross-cultural employee adjustment scale items were adapted according to nationality of cross-cultural employees.

Network characteristics. The interview findings suggested that employees develop social contacts and have social networks. However, the characteristics of these social networks were not revealed in the qualitative stage. In order to uncover the social network characteristics in this study, the 'name generator method' (Burt, 1992) was utilized. The name generator method has been widely used in previous social network research (cf. Bader & Schuster, 2015; Bruning et al., 2012; Wang & Nayir, 2006). Only initials of network partners were asked from respondents to address any reluctance of respondents to share their network members' (partners') names and to maintain the anonymity of these network partners. Network size was defined to be the number of partners in a respondent's network. Respondents were asked to provide the initials of people who had helped them in their jobs in the past 6 to 12 months. Respondents were asked to name a maximum of six people, as networks of three to four members are considered a significant size, as mentioned by Burt and his colleague (2017).

Responses were categorized on the basis of nationality and relationship of network members with each respondent. The categories included Chinese, Pakistani or other nationality employee (nationality), and whether the network member was in the same organization/project, an employee in a previous organization or a friend or family member (relationship with respondent). Employees in the same organization were coded as being part of a formal network, whereas employees in a previous organization, and friends and family were coded as part of an informal network. The sum of formal and informal networks was conditioned to be equal to network size of each respondent.

The network diversity was measured as the extent to which an employee's social network consisted of people from cross-nationality ties and was operationalized according to Wang and Nayir's (2006) study. Network diversity was calculated by multiplying the respective percentage of host versus home country nationals in an employee network. For example, if an employee social network consisted of four people, three of which were Chinese and one Pakistani, a score of $0.187 = [(3/4 = 0.75) \times (1/4 = 0.25)]$ would represent the network diversity. The maximum network diversity would be 0.25 and minimum would be 1 (indicating all the partners of the same nationality in the network of a respondent).

Network closeness and frequency scale were adapted from the study of Bader and Schuster (2015) and Wang and Nayir (2006). Network closeness (tie strength) was measured on a 4-point rating scale by asking employees to indicate how close they are to each person in their mentioned network (4=very close; 1=not very close).

Similarly, network frequency was measured on a 4-point rating scale as utilized in the study of Bader and Schuster (2015) by asking employees to indicate how often they contacted each network partner (4=daily; 1=quarterly). The higher values represented closer and more frequent relationships. In the interpretation of network closeness and frequency, the scores were summed up for each network partner in an employee network and the arithmetic average was calculated. For example, when the employee social network consisted of four network partners and an employee indicated 4 for the first person, 3 for second person, 2 for third person and 3 for fourth person, an average value of 3 was obtained for network frequency. The arithmetic average for network closeness was calculated in a similar manner.

Networking behaviour: Employees of both nationalities showed their networking behaviour intentions during qualitative interviews. Employees described their *guanxi* and *hawalas* development, which included formal (work-related) and informal (outside work) *guanxi* and *hawalas*. In a quantitative study, the boundary between inside and outside workplace is used to determine formal and informal networking according to Wolff and Moser (2006). The 18-item scale established by Wolff and Spurk (2020) was adapted in the present study. The scale is representative of the theoretically well-grounded, multidimensional nature of networking behaviours (Wolff & Spurk, 2020) and sufficiently identifies the networking behaviour. Moreover, the scale has provided a reliable, valid and economic measurement of networking behaviour in previous research (Wolff & Spurk, 2020). The scale has structural (formal versus informal) and functional (building, maintaining and using contacts) facets, achieved by combining two facets of Wolff and Moser's and Wolff and Spurk's derived subscales. These subscales are: building formal contacts, maintaining formal contacts, using formal contacts, building informal contacts, maintaining informal contacts and using informal contacts (see Appendix 2 for survey items).

Before the addressing the formal networking items, respondents were instructed to describe their behaviour in relation to colleagues in the same organization/project (formal). Similarly, before the informal networking items, respondents were instructed to describe their behaviour in relation to people who they knew but worked in other organizations (informal), including ex-employees and employees in different organizations. Respondents were instructed to select the relevant behaviour. For example, 'In my company, I approach employees I know by sight and start a conversation' (formal networking). Responses were recorded for both nationalities on a 5-point Likert scale (1=Always; 5=Never) and reliability was measured; well above acceptable rates were recorded, that is, $\alpha=0.93$ for Chinese, $\alpha=0.89$ for Pakistanis.

Cross-cultural employee adjustment: Cross-cultural employee adjustment was measured using a scale provided by Black and his colleagues (Black, 1988; Black & Stephens, 1989). The scale of 14 items, comprising three dimensions of employee adjustment, namely, general (seven items), interaction (four items) and work related (three items), was adapted for Chinese employees in the current study. However, since Pakistani employees were host country nationals, their adjustment was measured on the basis of interaction (four items) and work-related (three items) adjustment only. General adjustment was measured for expatriates since they relocate and adjust to general living conditions of the new country such as food, housing and other aspects (see studies by Black, 1988; Black & Stephens, 1989; Black & Gregersen, 1991; Black et al., 1992). For example, Chinese respondents were asked: 'How well adjusted (comfortable) are you to the living conditions in general?' (general adjustment). Similarly, both Chinese and Pakistani employees were asked: 'How well adjusted (comfortable) are you to the performance standards and expectations?' (work-related adjustment) and so on. An additional question relating to 'safety' was asked to measure the overall safety situation in the host country for Chinese employees. Similarly, Pakistani employees were asked about job safety and security in projects. Responses were recorded by both nationalities on a 5-point Likert scale (1= very much adjusted; 5= very unadjusted/very uncomfortable) for the above items and scale reliability was measured ($\alpha=0.89$ for Chinese, $\alpha=0.89$ for Pakistanis)

Project performance goals: Efficiency and effectiveness together measure the desired project performance goals. Although project performance goals may meet business goals (effectiveness), they may be over budget or exceed deadlines (efficiency) (Schmidt et al., 2001; Wang et al., 2006). Hence, project performance goals as a delivered project, depend on the achievement of business goals which are also within budget and on-time. The six items scale for project performance goals was adapted from the study of Wang et al. (2006) and Henderson and Lee (1992). Respondents were instructed to indicate their responses to how much they agree/disagree with each aspect of a project on a five-point Likert scale (1= strongly agree; 5=strongly disagree). For example, employees were asked to indicate their level of agreement to 'expected amount of work is completed as required', 'project/tasks adhere to schedule' and so on. The scale reliabilities for both nationalities were measured and deemed appropriate (α = 0.96 for Chinese, α = 0.85 for Pakistanis).

Conflict management: Conflict management was measured using a four-item scale adapted from the study of Rosenzweig and Roth (2007). In Rosenzweig and Roth's (2007) study, a systematic approach to collective handling of disagreements was developed through the involvement of all partners in the conflict resolution process. According to Rosenzweig and Roth (2007, p. 1315), conflict management is the 'joint responsibility' of employees and administration. Similarly, in this research the interview findings revealed that conflicts can be managed effectively when collective effort is made by employees at subordinate level and managers at supervisory level. Therefore, the survey included the items regarding conflict management as a collective responsibility of employees and organization. The same set of questions was asked to employees working in supervisory positions as well as employees at subordinate level. For example, employees were asked to indicate their level of agreement on a five-point Likert scale (1= strongly agree; 5=strongly disagree) to the following items: 'there are regular discussions among peers and supervisors for any difference of opinion' and 'settling of disputes is a joint responsibility between me and the organization'. The scale reliabilities for both nationalities were measured and deemed appropriate (α = 0.89 for Chinese, α = 0.76 for Pakistanis).

Communication satisfaction: The instrument used to measure communication satisfaction levels was adopted from the communication satisfaction questionnaire (CSQ) developed by Downs and Hazen (1977). The CSQ is based on a multidimensional scale, which is widely used in organizational contexts (Mount & Back, 1999). The scale comprises eight dimensions of communication satisfaction. However, for the sake of relevance in CPEC projects, two dimensions comprising communication climate (five items) and supervisory communication (four items) were utilized. Since other dimensions were not closely related, they were not included in the survey. Communication climate measures both organizational- and personal-level communication satisfaction. The organizational-level communication satisfaction is the extent to which communication inside organizations/projects motivates employees to achieve organizational/project goals. Personal-level communication satisfaction is the extent to which employees identify themselves with an organization and related projects. Supervisory communication measures the extent to which a supervisor is open to ideas, listens and pays attention to subordinates, and offers job-related guidance. The measure includes both upward and downward communication with supervisors. Hence, the scale can be equally utilized for employees in subordinate and supervisory positions. In addition to the two CSQ dimensions, an additional question was adopted from the Mount and Back (1999) study: "Overall, I am satisfied with the communication taking place in my organization". All the responses were measured on the five-point Likert scale (1=strongly agree; 5=strongly disagree). The scale reliabilities for both nationalities were measured and deemed appropriate (α=0.93 for Chinese, α=0.92 for Pakistanis).

Previous international experience: Employees of both nationalities were asked to indicate their previous international experience on an ordinal scale (Yes/No). The binary response was used as a tool to measure the proportion of employees in the samples who had experience of working in overseas assignments.

Language training and personal background: Language training was measured on an ordinal scale by asking employees of both nationalities whether they had received cross-language training after joining the project. This scale measured the initiatives taken in relation to training programmes in projects, as revealed in qualitative interviews. Chinese employees were asked if they received any English (Yes/No) and Urdu (Yes/No) training after joining the current project. Language training was measured by the average of English and Urdu training courses in the moderation model. Similarly, Pakistani employees were asked if they received any Mandarin training after joining the project (Yes/No).

Every respondent was asked background information, including gender, age, designation/position and company name in order to identify the sector of the company.

Hypotheses Development

As was found in Stage One of this study, the qualitative study findings provided rich information regarding Chinese and Pakistani employees' *social network* development and *networking behaviours* along with employee adjustment challenges and initiatives. The findings confirmed that employees of both nationalities utilized their networking and socialization skills for effective employee adjustment in the CPEC projects. The findings also confirmed that *employee adjustment* is important for *communication satisfaction* of employees, *conflict management* and successful achievement of *project performance goals*. However, the strength of relationships among the identified variables and how previous international experience and language training can help adequate adjustment, remained undisclosed. Moreover, the dimensional role of social networks, networking behaviour and employee adjustment remained unknown in Stage One. This aspect of the findings suggests the need for dimensional testing of the identified factors and measurement of the strength of these factors by the quantitative study. The findings and the relationship between the factors (i.e. social networks, networking behaviours, employee adjustment, communication satisfaction, conflict management and project performance) are integrated in the hypothesized model (see Figure 4.1). The following hypotheses reflect the logical thinking required to address the key question: What is the role of social networks and networking in cross-cultural adjustment?

H1: Social network diversity has a positive association with cross-cultural adjustment of Chinese and Pakistani employees.

H2: Networking behaviour has a positive association with cross-cultural adjustment of Chinese and Pakistani employees.

H3a: Formal networking behaviour is positively related to the general adjustment of Chinese employees.

H3b: Formal networking behaviour is positively related to interactional adjustment of Chinese and Pakistani employees.

H3c: Formal networking behaviour is positively related to work-related adjustment of Chinese and Pakistani employees.

H4a: Informal networking behaviour is positively related to general adjustment of Chinese employees.

H4b: Informal networking behaviour is positively related to interactional adjustment of Chinese and Pakistani employees.

H4c: Informal networking behaviour is positively related to work-related adjustment of Chinese and Pakistani employees.

H5a: Previous international experience moderates the relationship between social network size and cross-cultural employee adjustment.

H5b: Previous international experience moderates the relationship between networking behaviour and cross-cultural employee adjustment.

H6a: Language training moderates the relationship between social network size and cross-cultural employee adjustment.

H6b: Language training moderates the relationship between networking behaviour and cross-cultural employee adjustment.

Similarly, the following hypotheses were developed to answer RQ6: What are the impacts of employee adjustment and social networking on achieving project outcomes?

H7: Cross-cultural employee adjustment helps in achieving project performance goals.

H8: Cross-cultural employee adjustment is positively related to communication satisfaction among employees.

H9: Cross-cultural employee adjustment positively relates to conflict management in CPEC projects.

4.3 Data Collection and Analysis

The actual data was collected incrementally from April 2020 to August 2020 during personal visits to the projects and companies operating in Pakistan. As with Stage One of the study, companies from the transport, energy, construction, telecom and PSDP sectors were chosen. Since the construction sector includes energy and transportation projects, these projects were treated as a combined sector for the purpose of comprehension and analysis.

A total sample of 400 employees was selected, including both Chinese and Pakistani managerial-level employees working in the CPEC projects. Out of 400 targets, 253 surveys were returned with a response rate of 63.25 per cent and 4 surveys were discarded due to incomplete information or inadequate effort in responding.

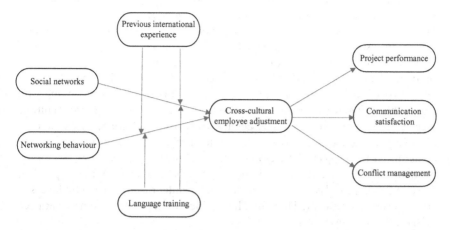

Figure 4.1 Hypothesized Research Model

Network metrics such as size, density and frequency can vary over time by increasing, decreasing or even remaining stable (Burt, 2020). Since the focus of this research was on understanding the network effects and networking behaviour of employees at a single point in time, cross-sectional research was suitable and thus adopted.

Data Screening and Analysis Technique

Before proceeding to data analysis, the data was screened for missing values, normality, outliers and assumptions of hierarchical regression. The data screening process ensured the suitability of the datasets (Chinese and Pakistani dataset) and that the datasets did not violate the assumptions of hierarchical multiple regression. In order to run hierarchical multiple regression and moderation analysis, the assumptions of linearity, data normality, homoscedasticity and multicollinearity were checked before analysis (Stockemer, 2019; Tabachnick & Fidell, 2007). It was important to take these steps so as to remove multivariate outliers and extreme cases. As an ex-ant (before distribution of survey) measure to address the multicollinearity issue and single common method bias according to Podsakoff et al. (2003), the independent and dependent variables were physically separated in the survey and an ex-post (after distributing survey) factor analysis measured multicollinearity using Harman's single factor test.

Multiple regression is the first-generation multivariate method, which is effective in gauging constructs and relationships between constructs (Tabachnick & Fidell, 2007). According to Tabachnick and Fidell (2007), N>50+8m, where m is the number of independent variables, represents the suitable sample size for regression analysis. After cleaning the data and deleting incomplete surveys, a total sample size of 240 was utilized for analysis. The sample size of both nationalities (Chinese=107, Pakistani=133) was deemed adequate for regression analysis. Hierarchical (sequential) regression is a type of multiple regression for multivariate analysis (Tabachnick & Fidell, 2007). In hierarchical regression, based on theoretical reasoning, multiple independent variables (IVs) can be regressed on dependent variables (DVs) in a sequence or hierarchy (Tabachnick & Fidell, 2007). As discussed in the literature review, social network diversity along with reasonable network size is important for employee adjustment in cross-cultural scenarios. It is believed that a larger network size with greater cross-cultural diversity among social networks will enable employees of both nationalities to adjust in CPEC projects. Therefore, social networks were treated as IV1 (independent variable 1) and employee networking behaviour as IV2 (independent variable 2). As postulated, together these independent factors help employees in cross-cultural adjustment. Therefore, hierarchical multiple regression was utilized in Stage Two of this research.

Although, structural equation modelling (SEM) is a parsimonious approach for model testing, SEM requires large sample sizes (i.e. greater than 250 for each group) to achieve effective model testing (Tabachnick & Fidell, 2013). Moreover, the chi-square test and fit indices improve with increased sample sizes, which make SEM a valid choice for larger samples (Hox & Bechger, 2001). Since the sample size of each nationality in this study was less than 250 and the main purpose of this quantitative study was to measure the relationships between the identified variables in the qualitative study and not model fit, SEM was not utilized in this study.

In order to measure the moderation effect of language training programmes and international experience on employee adjustment, the PROCESS MACRO technique by Andrew Hayes was utilized (Hayes, 2018). PROCESS MACRO is a computational procedure based on a path analysis framework, with the capacity to handle complex models involving multiple moderators and/or mediators (Hayes, 2012; Hayes et al., 2017). PROCESS MACRO produces a table of estimates of the indirect conditional effect of IV for various combinations of moderators (Hayes, 2018). PROCESS MACRO also produces a bootstrap confidence interval (CI) for inference of results (Hayes, 2018). As *a priori*, PROCESS MACRO does not allow latent variables, unless they have been reduced to observed variable proxies (i.e. sum or average of scores), which in this research have been reduced to observed variables (e.g. networking behaviour and employee adjustment). Moreover, PROCESS MACRO produces identical results to SEM for observed variable models. Thus, PROCESS MACRO was a suitable choice to avoid "greater effort and programming skill required to calculate relevant statistics and methods of inference (in SEM) that PROCESS does automatically and painlessly" (Hayes, 2018, pp. 80–81). Hierarchical regression was performed by means of IBM SPSS 23 and the PROCESS MACRO technique in SPSS was utilized for computation of moderation in this study.

Equivalence and Factor Analysis in Cross-cultural Studies

This study measured behaviours and associated data within a cross-cultural research context based on the assumption that differences in responses across the samples are due to cultural differences (Boer et al., 2018). The score differences can be misinterpreted due to a lack of comparability or measurement errors/ biases across samples of different cultures. The demonstration of measurement comparability as a prerequisite for cross-cultural comparisons, has been considered an integral aspect in previous studies (e.g. Steenkamp & Baumgartner, 1998; Vandenberg & Lance, 2000; van de Vijver & Leung, 1997). Measurement comparability in the present study determined the validity and reliability of scales across both cultures which were determined by measuring the Cronbach alpha (α). All the scales across both samples had a Cronbach alpha greater than 0.70; a Cronbach alpha of 0.70 or greater is considered an acceptable range (Nunnally, 1978). Hence, no items were deleted from the scales to improve scale reliability to an acceptable range (See Table 4.1 for scale reliabilities).

Validity was ensured by cross-cultural comparison of scales and elimination of biases. Three types of bias, including construct (theoretical concept), method (sampling, instrument and administration bias) and item bias (exploratory factor analysis with differential item functioning) can be found in cross-cultural studies (Boer et al., 2018). These biases can result in misinterpretation of results across samples. In order to manage these biases, this study determined three types of equivalence/invariance (i.e. functional, structural and measurement) to measure cultural differences across the Chinese and Pakistani samples (Vandenberg & Lance, 2000).

The similarity of psychological meaning of constructs across cultures was determined (functional equivalence) by exploration of variable terms. This approach included exploration of terms such as social networks (formal and informal), networking (formal and informal), *guanxi, hawala* and employee adjustment. The meaning of network structural facets (i.e. size, frequency and closeness) was also determined for functional equivalence. No direct statistical assessment for psychometric evidence of functional equivalence was performed; hence, qualitative exploration, document analysis and other non-statistical approaches, such as ontological comparisons of variables, were used to determine consistency of meaning for constructs across samples (Boer et al., 2018; van de Vijver & Leung, 1997).

Structural equivalence is determined if the theoretical construct is associated with the same observed variables across cultures (Boer et al., 2018). Structural equivalence was measured using the procedure adapted from Wuensch's (2016) study. The procedure uses exploratory factor analysis (EFA) with principal component analysis (PCA) as well as varimax rotation, to determine structural equivalence for the networking and employee adjustment scales and dimensions. As a prerequisite, Bartlett's test and Kaiser-Meyer-Olkin (KMO) measure of sampling adequacy was performed before structural equivalence was measured. Bartlett's test was significant and KMO was above 0.5. In order to measure Tucker's phi coefficient (i.e. r_c, a test of congruence by van de Vijver & Leung, 1997), each factor loading from the Chinese data (C) was multiplied by the corresponding factor loading in the Pakistani data (P). Then, the products were summed and were divided by the square root of the sum of squared loadings for the Chinese data, times the sum of squared loading for Pakistani data ($r_c = \sum CP / \sqrt{\sum C^2 \sum P^2}$). Tucker's phi coefficient was above the 0.90 threshold limit for factors of networking. In the case of employee adjustment, the coefficient was 0.85, where 0.85–0.94 are suitable ranges for Tucker's phi coefficient (van de Vijver & Leung, 1997; Wuensch, 2016). The comparatively low value of congruence for employee adjustment is attributed to the use of differently measured dimensions of employee adjustment (i.e. three dimensions for Chinese versus two dimensions for Pakistanis); this shows the variance for different dimensions of employee adjustment. This should not be perceived as bias or invariance as general adjustment was not measured in either sample. However, the interactional and work-related adjustments were measured as two separate dimensions for Chinese as well as Pakistanis. Hence, the procedure shows that structural equivalence prevailed in this study.

Similarly, measurement equivalence was determined using EFA which observes the comparison of factor loadings across cultures when employing unidimensional scales (i.e. conflict management and project objectives). The equivalence as shown in Table 4.1 explains the suitability of scales across both cultures, thus measuring the meaning of the same variables across both cultures.

Besides the need for equivalence in cross-cultural studies, EFA is the recommended procedure for determining the number of factors and the pattern of those factor loadings (Wolff & Spurk, 2020), since it helps in identifying if the variable has multiple dimensions and which items load on a particular variable and specific dimension. Since the items for all scales came from established scales in literature (Downs & Hazen, 1977; Rosenzweig & Roth, 2007; Wang et al., 2006; Wolff & Spurk, 2020) and none of the items were negatively coded, all items were entered into EFA. The solution generated three dimensions of employee adjustment for Chinese and two dimensions for Pakistan employees, as well as two dimensions of communication satisfaction for both Chinese and Pakistani employees. As the networking scale was reduced from 44 items to 18 items in Wolff and Spurk's (2020) latest research, EFA was utilized in the present research to further explore the dimensions in cross-cultural research. Interestingly, the networking scale initially generated a four-factor solution with PCA and varimax rotation with cross-loadings and within item multi-dimensionality with one factor with high loadings on formal network and negative loading on another factor. After consultation with Hans-Georg Wolff (developer of the networking scale), a Promax rotation with PCA and suppression of coefficients less than 0.3 criteria (Tabachnick & Fidell, 2014) was utilized as a criterion for a six-factor solution. Thus, the six-factor solution was found to be representative of two high order (formal and informal networking) and three low order (building and maintaining, using) factors. Similarly, for unidimensional variables the coefficients of less than 0.3 were suppressed and PCA was performed. The item loadings and reliability of scales are presented in the Table 4.1.

Table 4.1 Structural Equivalence Through Item Loadings and Scale Reliabilities

Variable	Items	Chinese Sample			Pakistani Sample		
		Loading	Variance Explained	Cronbach Alpha	Loading	Variance Explained	Cronbach Alpha
Networking Behaviour	In my company, I approach employees I know by sight and start a conversation	0.93	76.86%	0.93	0.64	69.55%	0.89
	I use company events to make new contacts	0.82			0.79		
	If I want to meet a person who could be of professional importance to me, I take the initiative and introduce myself	0.87			0.82		
	I catch up with colleagues from other departments about what they are working on	0.42			0.87		
	If I can't help a colleague from another department directly, I will keep an eye out for him/her	0.90			0.83		
	I discuss problems with colleagues from other departments that they are having with their work	0.85			0.73		
	I discuss upcoming organizational changes with colleagues from other departments	0.80			0.72		
	When I need answers to sensitive questions, I turn to reliable colleagues to find out more about the matter	0.36			0.79		
	At informal occasions I exchange professional tips and hints with colleagues from other departments	0.80			0.52		

(Continued)

Table 4.1 (Continued)

Variable	Items	Chinese Sample			Pakistani Sample		
		Loading	Variance Explained	Cronbach Alpha	Loading	Variance Explained	Cronbach Alpha
	I develop informal contacts with professionals outside the organization, in order to have personal links beyond the company	0.69			0.71		
	I use business trips or training programmes to build new contacts	0.84			0.53		
	When I meet a person from another organization who could be an important business contact for me, I compare notes with him/her about our common work areas	0.54			0.46		
	I meet with people from other organizations outside of regular working hours	0.91			0.79		
	I meet with people from other organizations that could be of professional importance to me at casual get-togethers	0.59			0.81		
	I use business events outside of the organization (trade shows, conferences) to talk to business acquaintances on a personal level	0.91			0.79		
	If I meet people from other organizations, I approach them to catch up on news and changes in their professional lives	0.62			0.77		

Construct	Item						
	I exchange professional tips and hints with people from other organizations	0.50			0.73		
	I confide in people outside of the organization for job-related matters	0.89			0.79		
Employee Adjustment	Living conditions in general	0.69	66.26%	0.89	N/A	N/A	N/A
	Housing conditions	0.49					
	Food	0.85					
	Shopping	0.85					
	Cost of living	0.61					
	Entertainment/recreation facilities and opportunities	0.84					
	Healthcare facilities	0.64					
	Socializing with cross-nationals	0.85			0.53	67.5%	0.89
	Interacting with cross-nationals on a day-to-day basis	0.91			0.9		
	Interacting with cross-nationals outside of work	0.81			0.68		
	Speaking with cross-nationals	0.85			0.90		
	Specific job responsibilities	0.63			0.56		
	Performance standards and expectations	0.43			0.96		
	Supervisory responsibilities	0.79			0.92		
	Safety	0.87			0.73		
Project performance goals	Project is able to meet the originally set project goals	0.87	78.5%	0.96	0.72	53.57%	0.82
	Expected amount of work is completed as required	0.91			0.77		
	High quality of work been completed	0.89			0.77		
	Project/Tasks adhere to schedule (deadlines)	0.91			0.81		
	Project/Tasks adhere to budget	0.86			0.58		
	Project efficiency of task operations	0.87			0.72		
Conflict Management	Systems and procedures are in place to resolve disputes among employees	0.73	68.5%	0.89	0.84	57.4%	0.76

(Continued)

Table 4.1 (Continued)

Variable	Items	Chinese Sample			Pakistani Sample		
		Loading	Variance Explained	Cronbach Alpha	Loading	Variance Explained	Cronbach Alpha
	Differences in opinion with other employees is an opportunity to improve relationship effectiveness	0.70			0.76		
	Settling of disputes is a joint responsibility between me and the organization	0.72			0.64		
	There are regular discussions among peers and supervisors for any difference of opinions	0.59			0.78		
Communication Satisfaction	Company/project communication motivates and stimulates enthusiasm for meeting project goals	0.79	78.5%	0.93	0.61	69.03%	0.92
	People in my project have great ability as communicators	1.0			0.98		
	Company's communication regarding project makes me identify with it or feel a vital part of it	0.81			0.78		
	I receive on-time information needed to do my job	0.95			0.84		
	Conflicts are handled appropriately through proper communication channels	0.39			0.72		
	Upper management listens and pays attention to me	0.63			0.51		
	My supervisor offers guidance for solving job-related problems	0.85			0.94		
	My supervisor trusts me	0.83			0.93		
	My supervisor is open to ideas	1.0			0.83		
	Overall, I am satisfied with the communication taking place in my company/project	0.38			0.66		

Descriptive Analysis of Chinese and Pakistani Samples

Demographic characteristics: The sample characteristics of Chinese and Pakistani employees are presented in Table 4.2. The sample comparison revealed that the majority of male employees were working in CPEC projects (Chinese 91 per cent, Pakistani 84.3 per cent). A greater number of female employees were working in projects in the Pakistani sample (16 per cent) compared to Chinese female employees (9 per cent) in the Chinese sample. In both sample groups, most employees were 26–30 years of age (45 per cent), followed by younger employees in the Pakistani sample (28 per cent of employees aged 20–25 years) and older employees in the Chinese sample (16 per cent of employees aged 31–55 years). The quantitative data indicated that Pakistani employees were mainly working as staff members in projects (75 per cent) and managerial positions were occupied by only 25 per cent of Pakistani employees. However, Chinese employees were mainly working in managerial positions (60 per cent).

Table 4.2 Demographic Characteristics of Chinese and Pakistani Samples

Demographic Characteristics	Number of Employees (N)		Percentage (%)	
	Chinese N=107	Pakistani N=133	Chinese	Pakistani
Gender				
Male	97	113	90.7%	84.3%
Female	10	21	9.3%	15.7%
Age (Years)				
20–25	13	37	12.1%	27.6%
26–30	48	60	44.9%	44.8%
31–35	26	21	24.3%	15.7%
36 and above	20	16	18.7%	11.9%
Designation				
Manager	64	34	59.8%	25.4%
Staff	43	100	40.2%	74.6%
Education				
High school	26	9	24.3%	6.7%
Bachelors	54	89	50.5%	66.4%
Masters	27	36	25.2%	26.9%
Language training				
Mandarin	–37	17—	34.6%	12.7%—
English	11		10.3%	
Urdu				
Previous International				
Experience	46	37	43%	27.6%
Yes	61	97	57%	72.4%
No				
Sector				
Energy & Construction	58	83	54.2%	61.9%
Telecom	45	31	42.1%	23.1%
PSDP	04	20	3.7%	14.9%

The majority of employees had bachelor degrees (Chinese 50.5 per cent, Pakistanis 66.4 per cent) and master degrees (Chinese 25.2 per cent, Pakistanis 26.9 per cent). Only 13 per cent of Pakistani employees attended Mandarin language courses and 35 per cent of Chinese employees attended English courses after joining the projects. Although the qualitative study findings revealed that companies were initiating language training programmes, as seen in the quantitative study results, very few employees had attended cross-language training.

Table 4.2 indicates that only 30 per cent of the employees in the Pakistani sample had previous international experience, as opposed to 43 per cent in the Chinese sample. Since energy and construction projects are a major portion of CPEC projects, the majority of employees of both nationalities were working in energy and construction projects, followed by telecom sector projects.

Network characteristics: In order to answer the question regarding the types of social networks and networking behaviours prevailing among employees working within the CPEC projects, the network composition characteristics, such as size, among others, were determined from the respondent's data and are presented in Table 4.3 along with mean and standard deviations (SDs) across both sample groups. Results showed that Pakistani employees had relatively large network sizes (mean=4.82, SD=1.69) compared to Chinese employees (mean=3.79, SD=1.95). The total network size of a respondent consisted of the formal and informal network, where Pakistani employees' informal network (mean=1.14, SD=1.48) was larger than that of Chinese employees (mean=0.72, SD=1.25). This suggested the important role of informal networks for Pakistanis (i.e. friends, family and previous colleagues) as an important element for work support activities in current projects. Similarly, network diversity showed that Pakistani employees had relatively higher diverse networks (mean=0.12, SD=0.11) compared to Chinese employees (mean= 0.09, SD=0.11), though both groups had a relatively lower level of diverse networks. Thus, Chinese employees with low network diversity preferred employees from their own nationality in their close network (see regression analysis in results Section 4.4). However, the network closeness and network

Table 4.3 Network Characteristics

Network Characteristics	Chinese Employees N=107		Pakistani Employees N=133	
	Mean	SD	Mean	SD
Network Size	3.79	1.95	4.82	1.69
Formal Network	3.07	1.88	3.70	1.80
Informal Network	0.72	1.25	1.14	1.48
Network Closeness	2.54		2.94	
(Tie strength)		0.95		0.67
Network Frequency	3.37	0.72	3.39	0.69
Network Diversity*	0.09	0.11	0.12	0.11

* Network Diversity value ranges from 0–0.25 where 0.25 is maximum diversity, between 0.12 and 0.20 as moderate diversity, and values close to zero have no/minimum diversity.

frequency were similar across both samples. See Table 4.3 for network characteristics data comparison.

Means Comparison for Networking Behaviour and Employee Adjustment

Mean comparison tests are performed as a prerequisite to determine if two sample groups share similar characteristics or are different (Hayes & Cai, 2007). A mean comparison test was performed in the present study to explore the differences between networking behaviour and cross-cultural employee adjustment among employees of both nationalities. As the sample sizes differed for the Chinese (N= 107) and Pakistani (N =133) sample groups, one-way ANOVA (Levene's test) with the Welch and Brown-Forsythe robust test for equality of means was deemed appropriate (Hayes & Cai, 2007; Tomarken & Serlin, 1986). ANOVA tests were performed separately for networking behaviour and employee adjustment, with nationality as a grouping variable to measure the differences. Levene's test of homogeneity of variance in ANOVA (Levene, 1961) showed that variances for networking behaviour across both samples were equal ($F(1, 238)=1.436$, $p=0.23$). Results revealed that there were no statistically significant differences between group means of networking behaviour (Chinese: mean=2.77, SD=0.70; Pakistani: mean=2.66, SD=0.72) as determined by one-way ANOVA ($F(1, 238)=1.344$, $p=0.25$). Both Welch and Brown-Forsythe tests are more robust than the standard F test of ANOVA (Tomarken & Serlin, 1986). The Welch ($F(1, 229.49) =1.351$, $p=0.25$) and Brown-Forsythe ($F(1, 229.49)=1.351$, $p=0.25$) tests were also found insignificant, suggesting that the overall networking behaviour of employees of both nationalities was similar. The networking behaviour here only measures the strength and existence of networking. It does not measure the criteria for initiating networking. Hence, the results of Stage Two regarding similarity of networking behaviour should not be considered contradictory to Stage One, which identified different criteria for initiating networking (*guanxi* or *hawala*) with potential partners. The ANOVA test, however, did not reveal the dimensional aspect of networking (formal and informal), nor the importance, which can be illustrated in regression analysis.

Levene's test showed that variances for employee adjustment across both samples were different ($F(1, 238)=4.972$, $p=0.027$). One-way ANOVA results revealed that differences between group means of employee adjustment (Chinese: mean=2.38, SD=0.61; Pakistani: mean=2.21, SD=0.78) were significant ($F(1, 238) =3.602$, $p=0.05$). The Welch test ($F(1, 237.691)=3.803$, $p=0.05$) and Brown-Forsythe tests ($F(1, 237.691)=3.803$, $p=0.05$) also supported the ANOVA test results, by revealing significant differences of employee adjustment among both nationalities. The mean comparison tests for employee networking and employee adjustment suggest that employee adjustment differs for employees of both nationalities although their networking behaviour is similar. However, the mean comparison test did not reveal the dimensional effects of each variable on both nationalities. Hence, it is important to further explore if employee networking results in similar employee adjustment for both nation-alities and which dimension (formal or informal) contributes more to employee adjustment. Dimensional correlation and regression analysis can reveal further insights while determining the relationship among other variables of interest as per the research questions.

4.4 Results

Variables Correlation Analysis

A variable correlation analysis is performed to measure the relationship among variables of interest (Tabachnick & Fidell, 2014). It also determines the range of relationship (–1 to +1) and direction (positive/negative) of relationship (Tabach-nick & Fidell, 2007). The key variable correlation in this study was measured by means of IBM SPSS 23. The correlation helps in determining if the relationship persists between variables of interest and can be further evaluated for causality in regression analysis (Hair et al., 2010).

With regard to the correlation among key variables, networking behaviour was positively and significantly correlated with employee adjustment in both sample groups (Chinese, r=0.23, p<0.05; Pakistanis, r=0.30, p<0.01). However, net-work size and network diversity were found to be insignificant in relation with employee adjustment in both sample groups, primarily because the employees preferred to secure support from their own country nationals, resulting in low network diversity. Hence, low network diversity was not related with employee adjustment. On the other hand, employee adjustment was significantly related to project performance goals (Chinese, r=0.37, p<0.01; Pakistani, r=0.49, p<0.01), communication satisfaction (Chinese, r=0.49, p<0.01; Pakistani, r=0.60, p<0.01) and conflict management (Chinese, r=0.29, p<0.01; Pakistani, r=0.51, p<0.01) in both sample groups. Moreover, the demographic variables were used as con-trol variables for the regression analysis. Table 4.4 presents correlation analysis among variables.

Moreover, in order to obtain in-depth insight into the variables, dimensional correlations were also performed for both sample groups. Table 4.5 shows the dimensional correlation analysis for both groups. In the Chinese sample, for-mal networking behaviour was significantly correlated to interactional (r=0.38, p<0.01) and work-related adjustment (r=0.20, p<0.05). However, formal net-working behaviour showed insignificant relationship with general adjustment in that sample. Moreover, informal networking behaviour showed insignificant rela-tionship with general, interactional and work-related adjustments for the Chinese sample. This finding supports the results of the qualitative study in which Chinese employees indicated that their professional *guanxi* (formal networking) was uti-lized for their employee adjustment and personal *guanxi* (informal networking) was utilized only outside work. General adjustment was significantly correlated with project performance goals (r=0.24, p<0.05) and communication satisfaction (r=0.41, p<0.01). Similarly, interactional adjustment was significantly correlated

Table 4.4 Correlation Analysis for Chinese and Pakistani Samples

Chinese Sample N=107

	Mean	SD	1	2	3	4	5	6	7	8	9	10	11	12	13
1 Gender	1.09	.29	1												
2 Age	2.50	.94	.002	1											
3 Designation	1.40	.49	.195*	-.252**	1										
4 Education	2.01	.71	.087	-.064	-.444**	-.015									
5 Previous International Experience	1.57	.49	-.110	.097	-.097	-.015									
6 Language Training	1.77	.33	-.125	.121	.009	.009	.186								
7 Sector	1.50	.57	.341**	.119	-.177	.478**	.026	.045							
8 Network Size	3.79	1.95	-.163	-.086	-.282**	.070	-.203*	-.189	-.174						
9 Network Diversity	.09	.11	-.077	-.093	-.249**	.178	-.036	-.015	.028	.551**	1				
10 Networking Behaviour	2.77	.70	-.022	.250**	.167	-.407**	.121	-.149	-.193*	-.023	-.211*	1			
11 Employee Adjustment	2.38	.61	.127	-.234*	.288**	-.245*	.025	-.061	-.298**	.057	.074	.225*	1		
12 Project Performance Goals	2.28	.88	.139	-.003	.312**	-.316**	.095	.222*	-.114	-.252**	-.113	.191*	.376**	1	
13 Conflict Management	2.30	.79	.110	.056	.178	-.218*	-.024	.216*	-.141	-.020	-.084	.168	.288**	.666**	1
14 Communication Satisfaction	2.21	.69	-.013	-.098	.362**	-.360**	-.083	.049	-.371**	-.091	-.020	.242*	.495**	.481**	.470**

(Continued)

Table 4.4 (Continued)

Pakistani Sample =133

	Mean	SD	1	2	3	4	5	6	7	8	9	10	11	12	13
1 Gender	1.16	.36	1												
2 Age	2.11	.95	-.052												
3 Designation	1.74	.44	.017	-.422**											
4 Education	2.20	.54	.225**	.192*	-.171*										
5 Previous International Experience	1.73	.45	-.154	-.463**	.419**	-.218*									
6 Language Training	1.87	.33	-.143	.046	-.069	.180*	.071								
7 Sector	1.53	.74	.221*	-.031	-.026	.250**	-.070	-.062							
8 Network Size	4.82	1.69	-.125	.144	-.175*	-.060	-.055	-.041	-.248**						
9 Network Diversity	.12	.11	-.275**	-.080	-.011	-.080	.018	.031	-.360**	.227**					
10 Networking Behaviour	2.66	.72	.194*	-.064	.098	.044	-.120	.059	.295**	-.295**	-.186*	1			
11 Employee Adjustment	2.20	.78	.034	.032	.055	.000	.020	.155	.089	-.061	-.058	.299**	1		
12 Project Performance Goals	1.95	.59	.235**	-.005	.102	.068	-.066	.051	.141	-.108	-.093	.453**	.490**	1	
13 Conflict Management	2.22	.78	.149	.048	.033	.005	-.159	.108	.024	-.087	-.058	.513**	.534**	.623**	1
14 Communication Satisfaction	2.01	.74	.021	-.053	.070	-.004	-.046	.177*	-.040	-.043	.131	.404**	.601**	.573**	.736**

** Correlation is significant at the 0.01 level (2-tailed).
* Correlation is significant at the 0.05 level (2-tailed).

with project performance goals (r=0.38, p<0.01), conflict management (r=0.41, p<0.01) and communication satisfaction (r=0.42, p<0.01). Lastly, work-related adjustment was significantly correlated with project performance goals (r=0.35, p<0.01), conflict management (r=0.24, p<0.05) and communication satisfaction (r=0.36, p<0.01).

In the Pakistani sample, formal networking behaviour was significantly corre-lated with interactional (r=0.29, p<0.01) and work-related adjustment (r=0.23, p<0.01). Similarly, informal networking behaviour was also significantly related with interactional (r=0.20, p<0.05) and work-related adjustment (r=0.28, p<0.01). This supports the results of the qualitative study as Pakistani respond-ents narrated their use of personal and professional *hawalas* (formal and infor-mal networking) for work-related activities. Moreover, interactional adjustment was significantly correlated with project performance goals (r=0.48, p<0.01), conflict management (r=0.47, p<0.01) and communication satisfaction (r=0.55, p<0.01). Work-related adjustment was significantly correlated with project per-formance goals (r=0.42, p<0.01), conflict management (r=0.51, p<0.01) and communication satisfaction (r=0.55, p<0.01). Hence, dimensional correlation provided evidence to pursue regression analysis for hypothesis testing of inde-pendent and dependent variables. Dimensional correlations along with mean and standard deviations for both samples are shown in Table 4.5.

Regression Analysis and Hypothesis Testing

Regression analysis was performed to answer quantitative research questions based on the hypothesized model shown in Figure 4.1.

In order to examine antecedents and consequences, hierarchical regression analysis was run for direct effects by means of IBM SPSS 23 for aforementioned hypothesis, as discussed in the following sections. For moderation effects, the PROCESS MACRO technique in SPSS was utilized. The model shown in Figure 4.1 includes: (a) direct effects of social networks and networking on employee adjustment; (b) direct effects of employee adjustment on commu-nication satisfaction, conflict management and project performance goals as a measure of positive outcomes; and (c) effects of language training and previous international experience of employees on employee adjustment. Models were accordingly estimated and statistically compared.

Chinese sample: Test of Hypothesized Model Including Moderation

The study collected 107 valid questionnaires from the Chinese sample of CPEC projects. Table 4.4 presents statistics and correlations among the variables used in hypothesis testing and model comparisons across the samples. A series of hierar-chical regressions was performed to assess the hypothesized model.

Direct effects: To test the direct effects of Hypotheses 1 and 2, a hierarchical regression was run. Step1 included control variables (gender, age, designation, education, training, international experience and sector). Step 2 was based on the

Table 4.5 Dimensional Correlation Analysis for Chinese and Pakistani Samples

Chinese Sample N=107

Sr.No.		Mean	SD	1	2	3	4	5	6	7	8	9
1	Formal Network	3.07	1.88	1								
2	Informal Network	0.72	1.25	-.273**								
3	Formal Networking	2.51	0.71	-.176	.048							
4	Informal Networking	3.02	0.82	.082	.003	.676**						
5	General Adjustment	2.51	0.74	.134	-.120	.115	.083					
6	Interactional Adjustment	2.35	0.86	-.114	.026	.385**	.148	.433**				
7	Work Adjustment	2.19	0.63	.193*	.066	.202*	.179	.499**	.528**			
8	Communication Satisfaction	2.21	0.69	.074	-.254**	.326**	.131	.413**	.419**	.363**		
9	Conflict Management	2.30	0.79	.021	-.063	.168	.141	.117	.407**	.241*	.470**	
10	Project Performance Goals	2.28	0.88	-.192*	-.105	.207*	.147	.238*	.379**	.349**	.481**	.666**

Pakistani Sample N=133

Sr. No.		Mean	SD	1	2	3	4	5	6	7	8
1	Formal Network	3.70	1.80	1							
2	Informal Network	1.14	1.48	-.490**							
3	Formal Networking Behaviour	2.47	0.63	-.163	-.067						
4	Informal Networking Behaviour	2.85	0.95	-.056	-.267**	.637**					
5	Interactional Adjustment	2.26	0.87	-.055	-.032	.298**	.204*				
6	Work Adjustment	2.15	0.84	-.014	-.050	.227**	.277**	.679**			
7	Project Performance Goals	1.96	0.59	-.036	-.092	.418**	.407**	.478**	.419**		
8	Conflict Management	2.22	0.78	-.045	-.052	.386**	.518**	.473**	.506**	.623**	
9	Communication Satisfaction	2.01	0.74	.009	-.080	.335**	.389**	.550**	.551**	.573**	.736**

**Correlation is significant at the 0.01 level (2-tailed).
* Correlation is significant at the 0.05 level (2-tailed).

literature review and measured the effect of network diversity on employee adjust-ment. As shown in Table 4.6, the direct effect of network diversity on employee adjustment was found to be statistically insignificant (β = 0.14, p=0.14). Thus, Hypothesis H1 was not supported. In Step 3, the effect of networking behaviour on employee adjustment was found to be statistically significant (R^2 =0.27, β = 0.23, p<0.05) and networking behaviour accounted for an additional variance in employee adjustment (ΔR^2 =0.04, p<0.05). Therefore, H2 was supported.

Hypotheses 7, 8 and 9 assume a positive relationship between employee adjust-ment and associated positive outcomes (i.e. project performance goals, commu-nication satisfaction and conflict management). The multiple regression results demonstrated that the effect of employee adjustment on project performance goals was significant (R^2 =0.30, β = 0.32, p<0.001), communication satisfaction (R^2 =0.37, β = 0.39, p<0.001) and conflict management (R^2 =0.19, β = 0.26, p<0.05). Thus, Hypotheses 7, 8 and 9 were supported.

Dimensional effects: The dimensional effects were measured for Hypotheses H3a–H3c and H4a–H4c. With regard to Hypotheses 3a–3c, after controlling the demographic variables, the effect of formal networking was found to be sta-tistically significant on interactional adjustment (β = 0.38, p<0.001) (H3b) and on work-related adjustment (β = 0.22, p=0.05) (H3c). However, the effect of

Table 4.6 Standardized Hierarchical Regression Coefficients for Network Diversity and Networking Behaviour Predicting Employee Adjustment

Predictors	Dependent Variable: Employee Adjustment		
	Step 1	Step 2	Step 3
	β	β	β
Gender	.21*	.22*	.22*
Age	–.19*	–.16	–.22*
Designation	.13	.16	.14
Education	–.08	–.09	–.02
Previous International	.08	.09	.06
Experience	–.05	–.03	.00
Urdu Training	.02	.01	.03
English Training	–.28*	–.28*	–.28*
Sector			
R^2	.22**		
ΔR^2	.22		
Network Diversity		.14	.17
R^2		.23	
ΔR^2		.02	
Networking Behaviour			.23*
R^2			.27*
ΔR^2			.04

Statistical significance: *p< .05; **p< .01; ***p< .001

formal networking was statistically insignificant for general adjustment ($\beta = 0.06$, p=0.52) (H3a). Hence, Hypotheses 3b and 3c were supported, while Hypothesis 3a was not supported.

Similarly, to measure the effect of informal networking on employee adjustment dimensions, namely, Hypotheses 4a–4c, the demographic variables were controlled. However, the effect of informal networking was found to be insignificant for all three dimensions of employee adjustment for the Chinese sample, that is, general ($\beta = 0.07$, p=0.43), interaction ($\beta = 0.09$, p=0.38) and work-related adjustment ($\beta = 0.19$, p=0.08). Thus, Hypotheses 4a–4c were not supported, suggesting that the qualitative findings which illustrated that the Chinese employees in the sample prefer to keep their professional and personal *guanxi*s separate while utilizing their personal *guanxi* (informal networking) only for personal tasks.

Moderation effects: The moderation effect on employee adjustment (Y) from network size (X) with previous international experience (W) and English training (Z) serving as a moderator of that relationship was measured by means of the PROCESS MACRO technique of Hayes (2012). Hypotheses 5a and 6a measured the relationship between network size as an independent variable (IV) and employee adjustment as a dependent variable (DV), moderated by previous international experience and language training. Both moderators were categorical and were recoded into 0,1 dummy variables (0 =No and 1=Yes) to have a meaningful interpretation for PROCESS MACRO. Model 2 was selected as a suitable model for double moderators (Hayes, 2013), and control variables, including networking behaviour, were added as covariates. Mean centering for network size was performed to facilitate the interpretation of regression parameters. Mean centering is the "act of subtracting a variable's mean from all observations on that variable in the dataset such that the variable's new mean is zero" (Iacobucci et al., 2016, p. 1308). It is advisable to perform mean centering when measuring main effects in addition to interaction terms and to remove non-essential multicollinearity (Iacobucci et al., 2016).

Results shown in Table 4.7 illustrate that overall, the model was significant (R^2 =0.3434, $F(12, 94) = 4.0970$, p<0.001). The interaction term for international experience (b=–0.1966, s.e.=0.0631, p=0.0024) and English training (b=0.1386, s.e.= 0.0621, p=0.0279) was statistically significant, thus, showing that binary international experience and English training moderated the effect of network size on employee adjustment. The effect of (centered) network size on employee adjustment was statistically insignificant (b=0.0697, s.e.=0.0440, p=0.1162). The regression slope for network size represents the relationship between network size and employee adjustment in the case of absence of English training and of previous international experience (coded 0). In short, there was an insignificant predictive relationship between network size and employee adjustment among employees who had no previous international experience and did not attend any English training after joining the project. Moreover, both previous international experience and English training on their own had an insignificant relationship with employee adjustment. Thus, Hypotheses 5a and 6a were

Table 4.7 Moderation Results of Network Size and Employee Adjustment for Chinese Sample

```
Model : 2
  Y : Emp.Adj
  X : NtSzCE
  W : Intl.Exp
  Z : EngTrn

Covariates:
 Gender Age Designation Education Sector UrduTrai Networking

Sample
Size: 107

****************************************************************
***************
OUTCOME VARIABLE:
 Emp.Adj

Model Summary
 R         R-sq      MSE       F         df1       df2       p
 .5860     .3434     .2742     4.0970    12.0000   94.0000   .0000

Model
             coeff     se        t         p         LLCI      ULCI
constant     2.1602    .6283     3.4379    .0009     .9126     3.4078
NtSzCE       .0697     .0440     1.5854    .1162     -.0176    .1571
Intl.Exp     -.0188    .1117     -.1679    .8670     -.2405    .2030
Int_1        -.1966    .0631     -3.1159   .0024     -.3219    -.0713
EngTrn       -.1211    .1208     -1.0020   .3189     -.3610    .1189
Int_2        .1386     .0621     2.2334    .0279     .0154     .2618
Gender       .3063     .2058     1.4881    .1401     -.1024    .7150
Age          -.1030    .0661     -1.5596   .1222     -.2342    .0281
Designat     .2174     .1390     1.5638    .1212     -.0586    .4935
Educatio     -.0459    .1026     -.4469    .6560     -.2497    .1579
Sector       -.2413    .1145     -2.1071   .0378     -.4686    -.0139
UrduTrai     .0007     .1908     .0036     .9971     -.3781    .3794
Networki     .1320     .0865     1.5272    .1301     -.0396    .3037

Product terms key:
 Int_1    :     NtSzCE    x     Intl.Exp
 Int_2    :     NtSzCE    x     EngTrn

Test(s) of highest order unconditional interaction(s):
          R2-chng    F          df1       df2       p
X*W       .0678      9.7088     1.0000    94.0000   .0024
X*Z       .0348      4.9879     1.0000    94.0000   .0279
BOTH      .0887      6.3480     2.0000    94.0000   .0026
----------
      Focal predict: NtSzCE   (X)
           Mod var: Intl.Exp (W)
           Mod var: EngTrn   (Z)

Level of confidence for all confidence intervals in output:
 95.0000
 ------ END MATRIX -----
```

supported by showing that network size in the presence of international experience and English training helps in employee adjustment.

Together, previous international experience and English training contribute a significant 8.87 per cent change in R^2 (R^2 change= 0.0887, F(2, 94) =6.3480, p=.0026).

Similarly, Hypotheses 5b and 6b measured the relationship between networking behaviour (IV) and employee adjustment (DV), moderated by previous international experience (W) and language training (Z). Model 2 was selected and control variables, including network size, were added as covariates. Mean centering for networking behaviour was performed to facilitate the interpretation of regression parameters. Results shown in Table 4.8 illustrate that the overall model was significant (R^2 =0.2564, F(12, 94) = 2.7016, p<0.05). However, the interaction term for international experience (b=−0.0524, s.e.=0.1871, p=0.7802) and English training (b=0.0914, s.e.= 0.2202, p=0.6789) was statistically insignificant. As binaries, international experience and English training do not provide in-depth information about years of international experience and level of training attended (basic, medium or expert level); the binary variables might not be sufficient to show their importance in networking initiatives and employee adjustment. Therefore, Hypotheses 5b and 6b are not supported in the Chinese sample of the current study.

Pakistani Sample: Test of Hypothesized Model Including Moderation

This study collected 133 questionnaires from employees in the Pakistani sample. The statistics and correlations of the sample are provided in Table 4.4. A series of hierarchical regressions as used in the Chinese case was performed to assess the hypothesized model.

Direct effects: In order to test the direct effects of Hypotheses 1 and 2, a hierarchical regression was run. Step1 included control variables (gender, age, designation, education, training, international experience and sector). Step 2 measured the effect of network diversity on employee adjustment. As shown in Table 4.9, the direct effect of network diversity on employee adjustment was found to be statistically insignificant (β = -0.008, p=0.94). Thus, Hypothesis H1 was not supported. However, in Step 3, the effect of networking behaviour was found to be statistically significant on employee adjustment (R^2 =0.12, β = 0.29, p<0.01). Moreover, networking behaviour also accounted for additional variance in employee adjustment (ΔR^2 =0.07, p<0.01). Therefore, H2 was supported.

Hypotheses 7, 8 and 9 assume a positive relationship between employee adjustment and associated positive outcomes (i.e. project performance goals, communication satisfaction and conflict management). The multiple regression results demonstrated that the effect of employee adjustment was significant on project performance goals (R^2 =0.30, β = 0.47, p<0.001), communication satisfaction (R^2 =0.39, β = 0.60, p<0.001) and conflict management (R^2 =0.34, β = 0.52, p<0.001). Thus, Hypotheses 7, 8 and 9 were supported.

Table 4.8 Moderation Results of Networking Behaviour and Employee Adjustment for Chinese Sample

```
Model : 2
    Y : Emp.Adj
    X : NtBeCE
    W : Intl.Exp
    Z : EngTrn

Covariates:
 Gender   Age    Designat Educatio Sector   UrduTrai NetSize
Sample
Size:   107

**************************************************************
***************
OUTCOME VARIABLE:
 Emp.Adj

Model Summary
    R       R-sq     MSE      F        df1       df2         p
  .5064   .2564    .3105    2.7016   12.0000   94.0000    .0036

Model
             coeff     se       t        p        LLCI       ULCI
constant    2.4162    .6431    3.7571   .0003    1.1393     3.6932
NtBeCE       .1702    .1128    1.5091   .1346    -.0537      .3941
Intl.Exp    -.0988    .1177    -.8391   .4035    -.3326      .1350
Int_1       -.0524    .1871    -.2799   .7802    -.4239      .3192
EngTrn      -.0522    .1330    -.3922   .6958    -.3162      .2119
Int_2        .0914    .2202    .4152    .6789    -.3457      .5286
Gender       .4478    .2134    2.0980   .0386    .0240       .8715
Age         -.1497    .0677    -2.2118  .0294    -.2841     -.0153
Designat     .1659    .1443    1.1497   .2532    -.1206      .4524
Educatio    -.0234    .1063    -.2199   .8264    -.2345      .1877
Sector      -.2790    .1220    -2.2869  .0244    -.5211 -    .0368
UrduTrai     .0196    .2159    .0910    .9277    -.4091      .4484
NetSize      .0260    .0325    .7994    .4261    -.0386      .0905

Product terms key:
 Int_1 : NtBeCE x Intl.Exp
 Int_2 : NtBeCE x EngTrn

Test(s) of highest order unconditional interaction(s):
        R2-chng    F          df1       df2          p
X*W      .0006     .0783      1.0000    94.0000    .7802
X*Z      .0014     .1724      1.0000    94.0000    .6789
BOTH     .0017     .1084      2.0000    94.0000    .8974
----------
   Focal predict: NtBeCE   (X)
           Mod var: Intl.Exp (W)
           Mod var: EngTrn   (Z)
Level of confidence for all confidence intervals in output:
 95.0000
------ END MATRIX -----
```

Table 4.9 Standardized Hierarchical Regression Coefficients for Network Diversity and Networking Behaviour Predicting Employee Adjustment

Predictors	Dependent Variable: Employee Adjustment		
	Step 1	*Step 2*	*Step 3*
	β	β	β
Gender	.0.6	.05	.02
Age	.09	.08	.11
Designation	.09	.09	.05
Education	− .07	− .07	− .05
Previous International	.01	.01	.07
Experience	.18*	.18*	.14
Mandarin Training	.11	.11	
Sector			
R^2	.05		
ΔR^2	.05		
Network Diversity		−.01	.01
R^2		.05	
ΔR^2		.00	
Networking Behaviour			.29**
R^2			.12**
ΔR^2			.07

Statistical significance: *$p < .05$; **$p < .01$; ***$p < .001$

Dimensional effects: The dimensional effects were measured for Hypotheses H3b–H3c and H4a–H4c. With regard to Hypotheses 3b and 3c, after controlling the demographic variables, the effect of formal networking on interactional adjustment was found to be statistically significant ($\beta = 0.28$, $p<0.01$) (H3b). Furthermore, the effect of formal networking on work-related adjustment was statistically significant ($\beta = 0.22$, $p=0.05$) (H3c). Hence, Hypotheses 3b and 3c were also supported in the Pakistani sample.

In contrast to the Chinese sample, the Pakistani sample indicated that the effect of informal networking on employee adjustment dimensions, that is, Hypotheses 4b–4c, was significant after controlling the demographic variables. The effect of informal networking was found to be statistically significant for interaction ($\beta = 0.18$, $p=0.05$) and work-related adjustment ($\beta = 0.27$, $p<0.01$). Thus, Hypotheses 4b–4c were supported in the Pakistani sample and confirmed the qualitative findings that Pakistanis utilize their professional and personal *hawalas* as and when required (interchangeably/overlapping) in personal and professional life.

Moderation effects: The moderation effect for the Pakistani sample between employee adjustment (Y) and network size (X) with previous international experience (W) and English training (Z) serving as a moderator of that relationship

Table 4.10 Moderation Results for Network Size and Employee Adjustment Pakistani
        Sample

```
Model : 2
  Y : Employee
  X : NtSzCE
  W : Intlexp
  Z : ManTrg

Covariates:
 Gender Age Designat Educatio Sector Networki

Sample
Size: 133

****************************************************************
 **************
OUTCOME VARIABLE:
 Employee

Model Summary
   R       R-sq      MSE        F        df1       df2        p
 .3680     .1354    .5815     1.7232  11.0000 121.0000  .0759

Model
             coeff       se        t        p       LLCI     ULCI
constant    .2657     .7597    .3498    .7271   -1.2383   1.7697
NtSzCE     -.1219     .2943   -.4141    .6796    -.7046    .4609
Intlexp     .0794     .1863    .4264    .6706    -.2894    .4482
Int_1      -.0721     .0938   -.7687    .4436    -.2579    .1136
ManTrg      .3542     .2127   1.6653    .0984    -.0669    .7753
Int_2       .1411     .1225   1.1520    .2516    -.1014    .3836
Gender      .0694     .1982    .3502    .7268    -.3230    .4618
Age         .0726     .0844    .8606    .3912    -.0945    .2397
Designat    .1210     .1804    .6707    .5037    -.2361    .4781
Educatio   -.0874     .1377   -.6352    .5265    -.3600    .1851
Sector      .0205     .1004    .2044    .8384    -.1783    .2194
Networki    .3214     .1030   3.1214    .0023     .1175    .5252

Product terms key:
 Int_1    :    NtSzCE   x            Intlexp
 Int_2    :    NtSzCE   x            ManTrg

Test(s) of highest order unconditional interaction(s):
      R2-chng    F       df1      df2    p
X*W    .0042    .5908   1.0000  121.0000     .4436
X*Z    .0095   1.3271   1.0000  121.0000     .2516
BOTH   .0146   1.0189   2.0000  121.0000     .3641
----------
    Focal predict: NtSzCE   (X)
         Mod var: Intlexp  (W)
         Mod var: ManTrg   (Z)

Level of confidence for all confidence intervals in output:
 95.0000
------ END MATRIX -----
```

Table 4.11 Moderation Results of Networking Behaviour and Employee Adjustment for Pakistani Sample

```
Model : 2
  Y : Employee
  X : NtBhvCE
  W : Intlexp
  Z : ManTrg

Covariates:
 Gender Age Designat Educatio Sector NetSize

Sample
Size: 133

*************************************************************
**************
OUTCOME VARIABLE:
 Employee

Model Summary
   R       R-sq     MSE      F        df1       df2         p
 .3482    .1212    .5910    1.5175   11.0000   121.0000  .1336

Model
              coeff     se       t        p       LLCI     ULCI
constant     .9505    .7909    1.2019   .2318   -.6152    2.5162
NtBhvCE      .2777    .6826     .4067   .6849  -1.0738    1.6291
Intlexp      .1291    .1905     .6777   .4993   -.2480     .5061
Int_1       -.0266    .2232    -.1190   .9055   -.4685     .4154
ManTrg       .3453    .2129    1.6217   .1075   -.0762     .7668
Int_2        .0505    .2829     .1784   .8587   -.5096     .6105
Gender       .0420    .1991     .2111   .8332   -.3521     .4362
Age          .0864    .0847    1.0203   .3096   -.0812     .2540
Designat     .0838    .1864     .4494   .6539   -.2853     .4528
Educatio    -.0654    .1387    -.4718   .6379   -.3399     .2091
Sector       .0414    .1023     .4049   .6863   -.1612     .2441
NetSize      .0181    .0428     .4219   .6738   -.0666     .1027

Product terms key:
 Int_1            : NtBhvCE  x            Intlexp
 Int_2            : NtBhvCE  x            ManTrg

Test(s) of highest order unconditional interaction(s):
      R2-chng      F       df1       df2          p
X*W   .0001     .0142    1.0000   121.0000     .9055
X*Z   .0002     .0318    1.0000   121.0000     .8587
BOTH  .0004     .0243    2.0000   121.0000     .9760
----------
 Focal predict: NtBhvCE  (X)
      Mod var: Intlexp   (W)
      Mod var: ManTrg    (Z)

Level of confidence for all confidence intervals in output:
 95.0000

------ END MATRIX -----
```

was measured using PROCESS MACRO. For Hypotheses 5a and 6a, network size (IV) and employee adjustment (DV) were moderated by employees' previous international experience and language training. Both categorical moderators were recoded into 0,1 dummy variables (0 =No and 1=Yes) to have a meaningful interpretation for PROCESS MACRO. Model 2 was selected for double moderators (Hayes, 2013) and control variables, including networking behaviour, were added as covariates. Mean centering for network size was performed to facilitate the interpretation of regression parameters. Results shown in Table 4.10 illustrate that the overall model was statistically insignificant (R^2 =0.1354, F(11, 121) = 1.7232, p=0.0759). The effect of (mean centered) network size on employee adjustment was also statistically insignificant (b=–0.1219, s.e.=0.2943, p=0.6796). Moreover, both international experience (b=–0.0721, s.e.=0.0938, p=0.4436) and Mandarin training (b=0.1411, s.e.= 0.1225, p=0.2516) were insignificant in demonstrating interactional relationship. Although the network size of the Pakistani sample was greater than that of the Chinese sample, it did not result in a significant relationship with employee adjustment. This finding suggests that network size may not represent network members' usefulness and contribution in cross-cultural interactional and work-related employee adjustment. Similarly, training and international experience as moderators showed insignificant interaction. Thus, Hypotheses 5a and 6a were not supported.

Hypotheses 5b and 6b measured the relationship between networking behaviour (IV) and employee adjustment (DV), moderated by previous international experience (W) and language training (Z). Model 2 was selected and control variables, including network size, were added as covariates. Mean centering in regression for networking behaviour was performed to facilitate the interpretation of regression parameters. Results shown in Table 4.11 illustrate that the overall model was insignificant (R^2 =0.1212, F(11, 121) = 1.5175, p=0.1336). Furthermore, the interaction term for international experience (b=-0.0266, s.e.=0.2232, p=0.9055) and Mandarin training (b=0.505, s.e.= 0.2829, p=0.8587) was statistically insignificant. Though direct effects show that networking behaviour improves employee adjustment (see Table 4.9), the moderation effects prove otherwise. Networking behaviour as a proxy of 'personal initiatives' may offset the benefits of language training and previous international experience of an employee. Therefore, Hypotheses 5b and 6b are not supported in the Pakistani sample of the current study.

Discussion of Quantitative Findings

The quantitative approach used for this study and described in this chapter makes a significant contribution to cross-cultural research by highlighting the types of social networks along with networking behaviour types, and their role in cross-cultural employee adjustment. This chapter examined the direct and dimensional effects of social networks and networking behaviour on employee adjustment. The moderating roles of binary previous international experience and language training on employee adjustment were also explored.

The results of the quantitative study are similar to those obtained in the qualitative study and demonstrate that most of the Chinese employees were working in managerial positions and most Pakistani employees as staff members. The quantitative study also showed that most of the male employees were employed in projects. A greater number of female employees in the Pakistani sample group were working in these projects compared to Chinese female employees. The finding is consistent with previous studies which have indicated that due to family issues and gender prejudice, the number of female expatriates (home country female employees) remains low compared to males and host country employees (Bader et al., 2018; Hutchings & Michailova, 2017).

Although structural theorists posit that some people are simply better positioned than others and thus benefit from a greater access to resources and work benefits (Burt, 2004; Burt & Soda, 2017; Lin, 1999), this quantitative study observed otherwise. The social network size and diversity in this study were statistically insignificant with regard to their relationship with employee adjustment and other positive outcomes. The reason can be twofold. First, it can be postulated that larger network sizes with greater network diversity are required for effective employee adjustment in a cross-cultural work environment. The smaller the network size, the fewer the number of contacts, which can lead to less social interaction and employee adjustment. Second, as revealed in the qualitative study, network development during projects is unclear and network membership is temporary within the work environment due to the dynamic nature of projects. Employees develop temporary or transactional-based network membership, with the aim of getting the work done during the projects. The term of transactional-based network is adapted from the study of Chaston (2000), where firms having a transactional or conservative marketing approach are either unable or unwish to form close collaboration with other firms in their market system.

In fact, project members do not have a farsighted approach for long-term relationship development mainly because most are contractual employees, as revealed in the document analysis, and are relocated to other projects after the commencement phase of the projects. Thus, the weak ties developed between cross-cultural employees do not result in strong ties over that period. Eventually, most employees do not recall (as was seen when asked during the survey) those weak ties or temporary network members as a part of their network. Social networks with a larger size, greater diversity and stable membership could be studied in future for associated benefits in cross-cultural assignments.

Despite the aforementioned phenomenon, the networks data revealed valuable information about the Chinese and Pakistani samples. Pakistani employees showed relatively greater network diversity, larger network size and larger informal network size compared to Chinese employees. Pakistani employees indicated a welcoming attitude in accepting Chinese employees socially and professionally as their network members, while maintaining professional closeness/distance with their Chinese counterparts. The low network diversity and smaller network size of Chinese employees may be explained by the shy nature of Chinese employees (Burt, 2019) causing them to mingle only with employees of the same nationality. Another reason for the low network diversity of Chinese employees may be the lack of host country network development and cultural norms, as explained in the qualitative interviews. The relatively small network size and smaller informal networks of Chinese employees compared to Pakistanis could also be explained by the status of Chinese employees as home or 'foreign' country nationals, where most have smaller networks based on their cautious approach towards employees from a different nationality.

This study indicated that employee willingness/initiative to socialize and interact (i.e. networking behaviour) is an important factor in cross-cultural employee adjustment (Wolff & Moser, 2009). In the quantitative study, the networking variable focused on measuring the 'building, maintaining and utilizing' of relationships developed for work or career. The networking behaviour of employees in the quantitative study reveals that efforts were maintained in developing relationships with other host and home country employees, which supported employee adjustment for both nationalities.

Further in-depth insights were revealed by employee dimensional networking behaviour, such as formal and informal networking (referred to as personal and professional *guanxi* and *hawala*s in the qualitative study). Employee formal networking was a significant contributor to work-related and interactional adjustment in the Chinese sample. This observation supports the qualitative findings that Chinese utilize professional *guanxi* for work-related adjustment in cross-cultural projects. However, the role of informal networking was found to be insignificant for interactional and work-related adjustment of Chinese employees. This observation also supports the qualitative findings that Chinese are mindful of utilizing their personal *guanxi* for non-work-related tasks. Hence, the results showed that Chinese employees utilize their formal networking for work-related tasks and informal networking for building rapport outside work.

The insignificant relationship of formal and informal networking to general adjustment can be explained by the Chinese preference to 'strive in cocoons' (Burt, 2019; Burt & Soda, 2017), their shy nature and utilization of professional *guanxi* being applied in work tasks only. These cocoons are only advantageous in early settlement (learning by observing) and in developing a comfort zone with nationals of the same country. However, these cocoons can become disadvantageous in long-term relationships with employees of other nationalities. Moreover, most of the general adjustment factors (e.g. food, life style and entertainment) for Chinese employees were regulated by the policies of the organization and Chinese embassy. Hence, general adjustment for the Chinese required less support from formal and informal networking in the current situation.

Besides greater network diversity in the Pakistani sample, the role of formal and informal networking was significant for work-related and interactional adjustment of Pakistani employees. It is thus evident that Pakistani employees utilize their formal and informal networking for building rapport, work tasks, comradeship and socialization with other employees. This finding is consistent with the study of Nadeem and Kayani (2019), which indicated that ethical *sifarish* (positive *hawala*s) can be utilized interchangeably with professional and personal purposes, such as for securing employment, securing a contract and/or admission in an educational institute.

The moderation effects of previous international experience and language training programmes on employee adjustment were partially supported in this study and was significant only for network size in the Chinese sample. However, the relationship was insignificant for the Pakistani sample which indicated a relatively larger network size. One can postulate that in the case of small network size, previous international experience and language training can help in employee adjustment by providing additional support. However, the language training programmes and previous international experience may be less required by employees already enjoying social support from larger networks. Further studies could measure these factors and their influences in more detail for different network sizes.

With regard to networking behaviour, the moderation effects were insignificant for both Chinese and Pakistani employees. Although meta-analyses show that previous international experiences, as well as training programmes, have a positive influence on cross-cultural adjustment (e.g. Bhaskar-Shrinivas et al., 2005; Burt & Soda, 2017; Deshpande & Viswesvaran, 1992), this study observed otherwise. The binary (Yes/No) previous international experience was asked in this survey. The binary responses concealed the quality of previous experiences of employees. The lack of information regarding the number of years spent in an international assignment and type of experience (work or non-work), explains the insignificant interactional relationship. According to the study by Moon et al. (2012), previous international experience includes the work as well as non-work-related experience of employees. The study also argues that employees' non-work-related experiences during previous assignments are sometimes more important to them (vacations or an argument with a local shopkeeper during a host country assignment) than work-related experiences. Employees also recall and report their non-work-related previous international experiences, which may not be useful in work adjustment to a new assignment. Moreover, according to Farr and Tippins (2013), previous international experience is useful only when the quality of this experience is positive and realistically and accurately aligned with the new host country norms and values.

Similarly, the binary (Yes/No) language training programme masked the level of training attended by employees. Information such as basic-, medium- or expert-level training, duration of training and refresher courses, are concealed in the binary responses. Hence, binary variables may not be sufficient to show the importance in networking initiatives and employee adjustment. Moreover, the didactic- and binary-level training programmes mostly reveal non-significant or partially negative results (Sit et al., 2017) and 'learning by doing' programmes may be more effective in cross-cultural adjustment. Thus, an advanced level of language proficiency and multiple training programmes may result in effective employee adjustment.

Some previous studies also indicated a non-significant relationship of language training and previous international experience with employee adjustment (e.g.

Hechanova et al., 2003; Shaffer et al., 1999). Therefore, mixed results are found in literature as well as in this study, for the role of previous international experience and training efficacy in employee adjustment. Further research is required to measure the multilevel language, behavioural and cognitive training programme effects on employees' cross-cultural adjustment along with previous international experience.

On a positive note, the project outcomes of communication satisfaction, project performance goals and conflict management showed positive relationships with employee adjustment, indicating that successful employee adjustment results in the achievement of communication satisfaction for employees and appropriate conflict management in an organization. Most importantly, cross-cultural employee adjustment also results in the successful achievement of project performance goal parameters. Hence, the networking behaviour and employee adjustment in both sample groups aided in achieving the CPEC project outcomes.

4.5 Summary

This chapter has presented the relationships among variables after the identification of key variables from Stage One of the study. The results supported the role of employee networking in employee adjustment. Consequently, employee adjustment significantly resulted in the achievement of effective project outcomes. It is observed that employee adjustment and networking behaviour of individuals are influenced by many factors. Thus, variations of networking behaviour (formal and informal) and employee adjustment in terms of culture, personality characteristics, organizational policies and implementation may lead to different employee responses. The next chapter presents a detailed discussion and a new framework by triangulating the findings from the qualitative and quantitative studies.

References

Bader, B., & Schuster, T. (2015). Expatriate social networks in terrorism-endangered countries: An empirical analysis in Afghanistan, India, Pakistan, and Saudi Arabia. *Journal of International Management, 21*(1), 63–77.

Bader, B., Stoermer, S., Bader, A. K., & Schuster, T. (2018). Institutional discrimination of women and workplace harassment of female expatriates. *Journal of Global Mobility, 6*(1), 40–58.

Bhaskar-Shrinivas, P., Harrison, D. A., Shaffer, M. A., & Luk, D. M. (2005). Input-based and time-based models of international adjustment: Meta-analytic evidence and theoretical extensions. *Academy of Management Journal, 48*, 257–281.

Black, J. S. (1988). Work role transitions: A study of American expatriate managers in Japan. *Journal of International Business Studies, 19*(2), 277–294.

Black, J. S., & Stephens, G. K. (1989). The influence of the spouse on American expatriate adjustment and intent to stay in Pacific rim overseas assignments. *Journal of Management, 15*(4), 529–544.

Black, J. S., & Gregersen, H. B. (1991). Antecedents to cross-cultural adjustment for expatriates in Pacific rim assignments. *Human Relations, 44,* 497–515.

Black, J. S., Gregersen, H. B., & Mendenhall, M. E. (1992). *Global assignments: Successfully expatriating and repatriating international managers.* San Francisco, CA: Jossey Bass.

Boer, D., Hanke, K., & He, J. (2018). On detecting systematic measurement error in cross-cultural research: A review and critical reflection on equivalence and invariance tests. *Journal of Cross-Cultural Psychology, 49*(5), 713–734.

Bruning, N. S., Sonpar, K., & Wang, X. (2012). Host-country national networks and expatriate effectiveness: A mixed-methods study. *Journal of International Business Studies, 43*(4), 444–450.

Burt, R. S. (1992). *Structural holes: The social structure of competition.* Cambridge: Harvard University Press.

Burt, R. S. (2004). Structural holes and good ideas. *American Journal of Sociology, 110*(2), 349–399.

Burt, R. S. (2019). Network disadvantaged entrepreneurs: Density, hierarchy, and success in China and the west. *Entrepreneurship Theory and Practice, 43*(1), 19–50.

Burt, R. S. (2020). *Structural holes: Capstone, cautions, and enthusiasms* [Working paper]. University of Chicago Booth School of Business. Retrieved 11 February 2020, from https://ronaldsburt.com/research/files/SHCCE.pdf

Burt, R. S., & Soda, G. (2017). Social origins of great strategies. *Strategy Science, 2*(4), 226–233.

Chaston, I. (2000). Organisational competence: Does networking confer advantage for high growth entrepreneurial firms? *Journal of Research in Marketing and Entrepreneurship, 2*(1), 36–56.

Deshpande, S. P., & Viswesvaran, C. (1992). Is cross-cultural training of expatriate managers effective: A meta analysis. *International Journal of Intercultural Relations, 16,* 295–310.

Downs, C. W., & Hazen, M. D. (1977). A factor analytic study of communication satisfaction. *The Journal of Business Communication, 14*(3), 63–73.

Farr, J. L., & Tippins, N. T. (Eds.). (2013). *Handbook of employee selection.* London and New York: Routledge.

Hair, J. F., Black, W. C., Babin, B. J., & Anderson, R. E. (2010). *Multivariate data analysis* (7th ed.). Upper Saddle River, NJ: Prentice Hall.

Hayes, A. F. (2012). *PROCESS: A versatile computational tool for observed variable mediation, moderation, and conditional process modeling.* [White paper]. Retrieved 20 March 2020, from www.afhayes.com/public/process2012.pdf

Hayes, A. F. (2013). *Model templates for PROCESS for SPSS and SAS.* [White paper]. Retrieved 19 March 2020, from www.personal.psu.edu/jxb14/M554/specreg/templates.pdf

Hayes, A. F. (2018). Partial, conditional, and moderated mediation: Quantification, inference, and interpretation. *Communication Monographs, 85*(1), 4–40.

Hayes, A. F., & Cai, L. (2007). Further evaluating the conditional decision rule for comparing two independent means. *British Journal of Mathematical and Statistical Psychology, 60*(2), 217–244.

Hayes, A. F., Montoya, A. K., & Rockwood, N. J. (2017). The analysis of mechanisms and their contingencies: PROCESS versus structural equation modeling. *Australasian Marketing Journal, 25*(1), 76–81.

Hechanova, R., Beehr, T. A., & Christiansen, N. D. (2003). Antecedents and consequences of employees adjustment to overseas assignment: A meta-analytic review. *Applied Psychology: An International Review, 52*(2), 213–236.

Henderson, J. C., & Lee, S. (1992). Managing I/S design teams: A control theories perspective. *Management Science, 38*(6), 757–777.

Hox, J. J., & Bechger, T. M. (2001). An introduction to structural equation modeling. *Family Science Review, 11*, 354–373.

Hutchings, K., & Michailova, S. (2017). Female expatriates: Towards a more inclusive view. In Y. McNulty & J. Selmer (Eds.), *Research handbook of expatriates* (pp. 241–260). Northampton, MA: Edward Elgar.

Iacobucci, D., Schneider, M. J., Popovich, D. L., & Bakamitsos, G. A. (2016). Mean centering helps alleviate "micro" but not "macro" multicollinearity. *Behavior Research Methods, 48*(4), 1308–1317.

Lavrakas, P. J. (2008). *Encyclopedia of survey research methods.* Thousand Oaks, CA: Sage.

Levene, H. (1961). Robust tests for equality of variances. In I. Olkin, S. G. Ghurye, W. Hoeffding, W. G. Madow, & H. B. Mann (Eds.), *Contributions to probability and statistics: Essays in honor of Harold hoteling* (pp. 279–292). Stanford, CA: Stanford University Press.

Lin, N. (1999). Building a network theory of social capital. *Connections, 22*(1), 28–51.

Moon, H. K., Choi, B. K., & Jung, J. S. (2012). Previous international experience, cross-cultural training, and expatriates' cross-cultural adjustment: Effects of cultural intelligence and goal orientation. *Human Resource Development Quarterly, 23*(3), 285–330.

Mount, D. J., & Back, K. J. (1999). A factor-analytic study of communication satisfaction in the lodging industry. *Journal of Hospitality & Tourism Research, 23*(4), 401–418.

Nadeem, S., & Kayani, N. (2019). Sifarish: Understanding the ethical versus unethical use of network-based hiring in Pakistan. *Journal of Business Ethics, 158*(4), 969–982.

Nunnally, J. C. (1978). *Psychometric theory* (2nd ed.). New York: McGraw-Hill.

Podsakoff, P. M., MacKenzie, S. B., Lee, J. Y., & Podsakoff, N. P. (2003). Common method biases in behavioral research: A critical review of the literature and recommended remedies. *Journal of Applied Psychology, 88*(5), 879–903.

Rosenzweig, E. D., & Roth, A. V. (2007). B2B seller competence: Construct development and measurement using a supply chain strategy lens. *Journal of Operations Management, 25*(6), 1311–1331.

Schmidt, R., Lyytinen, K., Keil, M., & Cule, P. (2001). Identifying software risks: An international Delphi study. *Journal of Management Information System, 17*(4), 5–36.

Shaffer, M. A., Harrison, D. A., & Gilley, K. M. (1999). Dimensions, determinants, and differences in the expatriate adjustment process. *Journal of International Business Studies, 30*(3), 557–581.

Sit, A., Mak, A. S., & Neill, J. T. (2017). Does cross-cultural training in tertiary education enhance cross-cultural adjustment? A systematic review. *International Journal of Intercultural Relations, 57*, 1–18.

Steenkamp, E. M., & Baumgartner, H. (1998). Assessing measurement invariance in cross-national consumer research. *Journal of Consumer Research, 25*, 78–107.

Stockemer, D. (2019). *Quantitative methods for the social sciences.* Cham: Springer.

Tabachnick, B. G., & Fidell, L. S. (2007). *Using multivariate statistics* (5th ed.). Boston: Allyn and Bacon.

Tabachnick, B. G., & Fidell, L. S. (2013). *Using multivariate statistics.* Boston: Pearson Education.

Tabachnick, B. G., & Fidell, L. S. (2014). *Using multivariate statistics* (6th ed.). Harlow: Pearson.

Tomarken, A. J., & Serlin, R. C. (1986). Comparison of ANOVA alternatives under variance heterogeneity and specific noncentrality structures. *Psychological Bulletin, 99*(1), 90.

van de Vijver, F. J. R., & Leung, K. (1997). *Methods and data analysis of comparative research.* Thousand Oaks, CA: Sage.

Vandenberg, R. J., & Lance, C. E. (2000). A review and synthesis of the measurement invariance literature: Suggestions, practices, and recommendations for organizational research. *Organizational Research Methods, 3,* 4–70.

Wang, E. T., Wei, H. L., Jiang, J. J., & Klein, G. (2006). User diversity impact on project performance in an environment with organizational technology learning and management review processes. *International Journal of Project Management, 24*(5), 405–411.

Wang, X., & Nayir, D. Z. (2006). How and when is social networking important? Comparing European expatriate adjustment in China and Turkey. *Journal of International Management, 12*(4), 449–472.

Wolff, H.-G., & Moser, K. (2006). Entwicklung und validierung einernetworkingskala [Development and validation of a networking scale]. *Diagnostica, 52,* 161–180.

Wolff, H.-G., & Moser, K. (2009). Effects of networking on career success: A longitudinal study. *Journal of Applied Psychology, 94*(1), 196–206.

Wolff, H.-G., & Spurk, D. (2020). Developing and validating a short networking behavior scale (SNBS) from Wolff and Moser's (2006) measure. *Journal of Career Assessment, 28*(2), 277–302.

Wuensch, K. L. (2016). *Comparing two groups' factor structures: Pearson r and the coefficient of congruence.* Retrieved 8 May 2020, from http://core.ecu.edu/psyc/wuenschk/MV/FA/FactorStructure-TwoGroups.docx

5 Conclusion

5.1 Introduction

An increasing trend of cross-cultural challenges is being faced by organizations and employees alike, particularly among newly emerging MNEs and their employees. Our case studies taken from BRI and CPEC projects demonstrate that the effective mechanisms to achieve good outcomes for organizations and well-being for individuals consist of supportive work environments with effective social networks (Wang & Nayir, 2006) and the related efforts made by both organizations and employees. In this concluding chapter, we focus on two important aspects, namely: (1) the overall lessons learnt from the BRI and CPEC projects regarding cross-cultural management challenges for companies as well as cross-cultural adjustments for employees and (2) implications for further conceptual understanding regarding cross-cultural management, social networks, networking behaviour and other pertinent issues. This chapter concludes with a discussion on future research directions in the areas of managing international collaborative projects in general and projects under the BRI and CPEC.

5.2 Drawing Lessons From the BRI and CPEC Projects

On the basis of our research findings, we can draw on a number of important lessons for future development of the BRI in general and the CPEC projects in particular. Peter M. Blau pointed out (see Durbin, 2011, p. 92), "structures of objective social positions, among which people are distributed, exert a more fundamental influence on social life than do cultural values and norms". The situation has changed paradoxically in emerging economies where cross-cultural collaborative projects are emerging. Therefore, key lessons for governments, organizations and individual employees involved in international collaborative projects should be drawn in order to improve the development of future projects.

Lessons for Governments

A number of challenging issues were discovered in this research regarding the role of governments for both countries studied, such as the need for more supportive

DOI: 10.4324/9781003240815-5

government policies at multiple levels regarding investment, infrastructure development, frequent cross-cultural dialogues and security. In this regard, the successful development of multimillion-dollar projects depends on the governments of both countries implementing policies to benefit cross-cultural and cross-country projects with investment in the BRI and CPEC. For example, both governments should develop a comprehensive system to ease business operations in industrial clusters and special economic zones (SEZs), such as aligning trade and industrial policies and single window operations for business approvals in the host country with home country government support.

In addition, policymakers of both countries should strengthen and standardize mentoring and training programmes, ensuring that organizations make language, behavioural and skill-based training mandatory for relevant employees. Organizations would thus be in a position to comply with government rules when initiating their businesses in cross-cultural projects. Mentoring is another neglected area of CPEC projects and requires an affirmative policy. It should be mandatory for operating companies to assign a senior employee (who has worked internationally) as a mentor to new employees of different nationalities working on projects, thus allowing for cross-cultural psychological/social connections among employees by reducing misunderstandings arising from cultural and communication differences.

Governments should also implement specific policy amendments. For example, given the economic and strategic importance of the CPEC projects, the Chinese government should address cross-cultural issues seriously by establishing frequent cultural exchange programmes, policymaking dialogue between both countries' management teams and regular briefing between organizational management teams and government representatives aimed at promoting cultural affinity.

Similarly, given the significance of the CPEC projects in national development through strong infrastructure and new industrial capabilities, the Pakistani government should reform its governing system to ease the approval of new CPEC projects with fewer bureaucratic procedures. A number of issues, such as the approval of new projects, attracting new investment opportunities, developing cultural exchange initiatives and cross-cultural language training, require further government support. For example, centrally supervised training institutes at different government levels and 'one-stop-shops' for business approvals in SEZs and elsewhere would enable the effective implementation of the relevant programmes and business operations.

Lessons for Organization Policy and Management Practices

The challenging issues faced by organizations, such as lack of cross-cultural knowledge and language competency among employees, absence of national diversity at managerial levels, homophily in social networks and lack of empathy towards cross-cultural work norms, require more effective policy and management practices to improve the situation. For this reason, integral reforms are required at company level with training and mentoring programmes, cross-cultural network development, HR policies for employee selection, employee development and continuous adjustment assistance.

Training and Mentoring

Generally speaking, as shown throughout this research, the language barrier is the major obstacle for Chinese employees in developing close bonds with Pakistani colleagues. Organizational efforts should be directed towards removing this barrier between the two nationalities through greater administrative support of cultural and language training programmes and extracurricular activities such as field trips. Language training programmes can be useful if they are comprehensive and can improve communication efficiency and satisfaction among employees of different nationalities. Furthermore, language courses can yield beneficial results when combined with specific cognitive and behavioural training programmes. For example, cognitive adjustment may be effectively promoted through 'cultural diffusion' training programmes whereby individuals are presented with multiple cultural scenarios in order to identify misunderstandings, as well as responses to different behaviours and alternative actions and rationales.

Cross-cultural trainers, along with managers, are integral to the improvement of language and cultural competence for the delivery of need-based training in the pre- and post-departure phases of expatriate employees. These training programmes can eventually improve the cross-cultural skills and language capabilities among both host and home country employees and smooth future cultural interactions.

Cross-Cultural Network Development

From the structural perspective of networks, organizational policy should focus on cross-cultural network brokers who could be language interpreters working in the organization, bilingual managers and cross-cultural mentors, acting as integral facilitators for cross-cultural network development. Network brokers are an invaluable asset for managing cross-cultural conflict and should be carefully selected from among those who are considered trustworthy by cross-nationality individuals and have cross-cultural knowledge. These network brokers can enable intermingling of two separate groups by translating opinions and behaviours between one party and another using a familiar manner and dialect. This heterophily could enable both Chinese and Pakistani employees to mitigate their psychological and cultural networking barriers.

We also suggest that expatriate managers should be sensitive to differences among employees, their individual mental and cultural patterns, and characteristics. These managers must have strong cross-cultural management capabilities, flexible attitudes, willingness to relocate and previous international work experience; these attributes should be key criteria for selecting people for international assignments.

Furthermore, the current research also highlights the responsibility of organizations and managers in dealing with both nationalities of employees in a geocentric fashion. Organizational policy should enable global managers to analyse the nature of the social networks, identify gatekeepers/influencers of those networks and motivate them to create a networking ripple effect in the network. The gate keepers/influencers would act as a facilitating force for the socialization of network members, thus enhancing employees' communication satisfaction. Furthermore, in order to make employees feel at home, a dedicated formal effort is required from the managerial side to create and adequately support cross-cultural workgroups. Thus, connecting and working together with cross-cultural employees can help mitigate loneliness for Chinese employees and encourage them to establish friendships with Pakistani employees.

HR Policies for Employee Selection and Development

Obtaining and building cross-cultural competences among employees of both nationalities are challenging issues which require particular attention from the HR management department. With regard to selecting expatriates (i.e. Chinese in this study), a pre-departure analysis should be carried out to assess an individual's capabilities, family-related issues and willingness to relocate to a new country.

A pre-departure analysis to assess relevant skills, knowledge and ability to handle different cultural norms, would enable organizations to ensure the success of employee adjustment and associated challenges in a new cultural environment. Furthermore, policies designed to support family accompaniment of expatriates could improve social and emotional wellbeing and cultural competence, and thus may lead to better employee adjustment. At the same time, willingness to relocate to a new assignment in a different country is also an important factor for cross-cultural employee adjustment and can lead to associated positive outcomes. Hence, employees who are specifically willing to relocate should be selected for such international assignments in the future. In addition, ongoing support during the period of the overseas assignment is required, such as providing cultural understanding and language training as well as mentoring support, communicating regularly regarding daily challenges and addressing issues affecting work and family life.

Cultural competences are equally important with regard to the local employees (i.e. Pakistani in this study). The HR management department should also pay attention to recruiting people with cultural adaptability and provide ongoing training and mentoring accordingly.

Besides the duration of projects and willingness of employees, status (supervisor or subordinate) is also a factor for homophily, as backed by the interview data. Chinese employees' homophily is associated with the inhibition of Pakistani employees to socialize with them due to the supervisor-subordinate relationships. As majority of the CPEC projects are operated by Chinese EMNEs, Chinese employers enjoy preferential treatment in administrative cadre positions and decision-making. Most of the Chinese employees are working on administrative positions with more power while Pakistani employees as team members and team leaders, which created complexities for Pakistani employees given their subordinate position at workplace. There is a strong need to balance the power dependence relationship between Chinese employers and Pakistani employees and a balanced approach within administrative cadre nationalities, so that Pakistani employees feel equally important at workplace. Hence, it is suggested that HR departments should also promote Pakistani employees based on merit to managerial levels. By virtue of this, both sides can understand the lacuna of specifics and will result in an understanding of workplace dynamics.

Implications for Individuals

Besides organizational implications, the current research also offers a set of implications for home and host country employees who need to understand the importance of social interactions and networking, show empathy towards cross-cultural employees' work habits and build trust among employees with different cultural backgrounds.

Social Interaction and Networking

The influence of cultural norms on employee networking and social network development has a noticeable effect on cross-cultural adjustment and achievement of positive outcomes by employees. Building diverse social networks and trusting relationships may be a slow and steady process, which requires frequent interactions between host and home country employees through observations of the new culture, adaptation to new work and cultural norms and language compatibility.

Since Chinese employees have a relatively small network base and low network diversity in a foreign country, as well as a short-term approach to work through projects as transactional networking, these factors could jeopardize the development of substantial cross-cultural networks and negatively influence the progress of cross-country collaborative projects. Therefore, both managers and employees need to be aware of such problems and commit to instrumental networking behaviour with long-term orientation for ongoing development.

Employee Work Habits

Our study has identified that Chinese managers have been seen as 'workaholics' by Pakistani employees, are also considered to be high achievers. Hence, other hard-working Pakistani employees may be more attractive to those Chinese managers and may thus be included in their networks, resulting in social refusal of lower achievers of Pakistani employees as perceived by those Chinese managers. Given that the work attitude and behaviour of Pakistani employees differ from those of Chinese managers, a mental barrier may exist for Chinese managers to accept many Pakistani employees into their social networks. It is important for

Chinese in management positions to be aware of this barrier and act accordingly to overcome it.

On the other hand, in order to 'fit-into' the social network criteria of Chinese managers, Pakistani employees may also need to adjust their work attitude and behaviour accordingly with the support of Chinese managers in order to improve skills and abilities among Pakistani employees. Chinese employees must make efforts to overcome their 'outsider' status by congenial approach towards relationship building and flexibility to work norms of local employees (Guo et al., 2018). This will enable Chinese employees to develop a local clan and family of friends away from their home country. By developing a win-win situation for both nationalities, the objectives of the CPEC projects can be achieved with fewer obstacles.

Cognitive Reconstruction

The findings of this study indicate interesting implications for the behavioural aspects of networks. For instance, there is a strong need for employees to develop trust between different nationalities to build strong network connections. To recapitulate, government policies, organizational initiatives and, in particular, home and host country employees' initiatives can help employees in cross-cultural engagement and adequate adjustment, where acceptance of change is the first step. The 'us vs. them' mental model (Guo et al., 2021) needs to be changed to 'we' approach, by prioritizing cross-cultural language training programmes, cultural sensitivity and diverse networking in projects. Therefore, by allowing individuals to address cross-cultural challenges and by identifying networking opportunities for building strong personal and professional engagements under the guidance of experienced mentors, individuals of both nationalities can overcome those cross-cultural challenges.

5.3 Implications for Cross-Cultural Management, Network and Networking Behaviour

Based on the discussion of the major findings of this research, a number of conceptual implications for cross-cultural management, network and networking behaviour can be highlighted here.

The main implication concerns the development of a holistic conceptual framework. As Figure 5.1 demonstrates, there are a number of important interactive factors influencing the entire process of cross-cultural projects. The framework highlights the cultural tensions arising due to Chinese and Pakistani employee interaction with different values, attitudes and behaviour. There are also a number of organizational and individual factors affecting employee cross-cultural adjustment and achieving project objectives. Issues such as diverse social networks, employee networking initiatives, family support, international experience, language proficiency, flexibility of working time, ample socialization opportunities, cultural similarity and affinity, training and mentoring programmes, as well

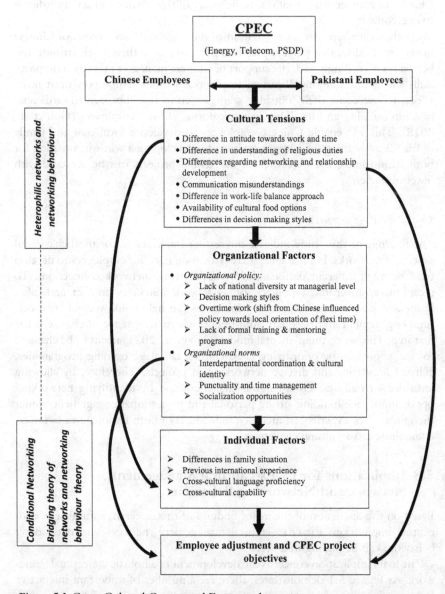

Figure 5.1 Cross-Cultural Conceptual Framework

as individual's proactiveness and openness to experience, are key contributing factors towards adequate cross-cultural employee adjustment and subsequently achieving project objectives. Lack of any of these could result in an individual's frustration and stress, and inefficiency in completing tasks. In addition, adequate cross-cultural adjustment helps in mitigating perceptual cultural differences between employees over time, and eventually improving human bonding and relationships building. Employee adjustment is a tedious process which takes time and requires proactiveness from all parties concerned (individuals, colleagues, and organization). Therefore, our new framework complements the current fragmented social network literature by providing a holistic view of network structure and behaviour along with supportive factors. This framework also links the structural and behavioural view of networks by using a joint measurement of social network characteristics and networking behaviour.

Another implication is related to the concept of *contextual/conditional networking behaviour*. Our findings support the notion that cross-cultural networking is a context/condition-driven behaviour, where multiple conjoined factors play an important role in the process of network development and influence the networking behaviour, such as different cultural and institutional differences (Savani et al., 2011).

Contrary to previous studies which advocate the integral utility of social networks structural view (see, for example, Burt, 1992; Burt et al., 2013, Granovetter, 1973; Gulati, 1998; Gulati et al., 2000, Lin, 1999a, 1999b, 2001), this research concludes that the behavioural component of social networks (i.e. networking behaviour) is more influential in dynamic cross-cultural projects. This was evident from Stage Two results which indicated a positive relationship of networking behaviour to employee adjustment and lack of observed relationship between social networks and employee adjustment in Chinese and Pakistani sample groups. A similar finding was observed in Stage One of the research where social networks were underutilized to generate associated positive outcomes. Future studies can further verify the dominance of networking behaviour over social networks to verify these research findings.

A further implication is related to the composition of Chinese social network structures in non-homogenous cultural projects. According to Burt and Burzynska (2017), mixed evidence was found of denser Chinese in-group networks or structural holes in homogenous cultures, revealing that even in cross-cultural projects, Chinese social networks are characterized by denser, more homogeneous and trustworthy members, thus lacking diversity. The present research observed that low network diversity of Chinese employees' social networks inhibits their cross-cultural employee adjustment. This research has thus not only advanced the study of Burt and Burzynska (2017) by studying Chinese network structures in a heterogeneous cultural environment, but also provided additional evidence that social networks comprise the same nationality even in heterogeneous cultures. Hence, it is important to point out that employees connected to multiple separate and ethnic groups are likely to see the value of work being coordinated between different cultural groups (Burt, 2010; Burt et al., 2000). These employees would be able to identify potential valuable new employees to be included in future projects based on their connections. However, recognition of diverse knowledge is one thing and acquisition of diverse knowledge is another (Soda et al., 2018). Willingness is integral to employees building cross-cultural networks between different nationalities.

Furthermore, this research provides meaningful implications for the culturally limited networking behaviour literature, through a comparison of the networking phenomenon between two different Asian cultures. The research findings compare the ontological and epistemological significance of informal networking across Chinese and Pakistani cultures. Ontological similarities prevail among *guanxi* and *hawala*, but contextually Chinese professionalism inhibits Chinese employees in utilizing their personal *guanxi* for professional work. Although the negative connotation of *sifarish* (nepotism) with *hawalas* and *rent-seeking behaviour* with *guanxi* prevails, the benefits of positive *guanxi* and *hawalas* outweigh the negative elements. From school admission to job promotion (Islam, 2004), as well as in gaining confidence in the eyes of a supervisor, *hawalas* from a resourceful supervisor can benefit a common Pakistani who does not have access to upper tiers of decision-makers. Similarly, *guanxi* benefits Chinese employees in securing bonuses and promotions (Chen at al., 2009). The Chinese professional *guanxi* focuses on the quality of the professionalism and trustworthy character of individuals as criteria for forming networks, but Pakistanis *hawalas* emphasize personal and social connections rather than professional capabilities in forming network. Thus, employees from two neighbouring countries work together on CPEC projects but behave differently in their social interactions.

Lastly, implications for cross-cultural employee adjustment are also important. The concept of cross-cultural employee adjustment should be more than a 'psychological adjustment' or 'reaching the general satisfaction in the new environment', as defined in the literature (Black et al., 1992; Hechanova et al., 2003). The present research demonstrates that cross-cultural employee adjustment is a *cognitive reconstruction* towards diverse cultural perceptions, social interactions, work norms, and societal and religious value systems. This research provides a compelling evidence that cognitive reconstruction relates to the acceptance of culturally influenced views of employees of another nationality. This cognitive reconstruction is equally important for both host and home country employees regardless of their home or host country status. The reconstruction requires recognition and development of an individual's personal views in response to the surrounding environment, and postulates learning by experience and being resilient to different work and networking norms. Adequate employee adjustment, as in cognitive reconstruction, could build resilience among employees in uncertain situations and promote flexibility in the presence of communication challenges. Employee adjustment could also enhance the development of a positive mindset and tolerant attitude towards different work norms and habits; moreover, it could allow expatriate employees to identify cognitive distortions and rationally adapt to a changing environment. As a result of rational thinking and adaptation, a trust relationship could be developed between cross-nationality employees.

5.4 Concluding Remarks

In developing this research, the focus has been on exploring relevant cross-cultural issues in the CPEC projects and the ways social networks and networking behaviour can help in employee adjustment. However, there are a number of limitations in this research and further study is required to address these issues.

First, this research has identified the important role of cross-cultural mentors and network brokers in one particular country, namely Pakistan. Future research could cover multiple countries by analysing the role of global network members. These members include people working in similar projects in different countries, industry acquaintances and other online members of networks (Seibert et al., 2001). These members are not directly related to projects but aid employees by giving suggestions and guidance. Future research could measure the broader social networks of employees in multiple countries. Moreover, it is possible that employees' networking behaviour may affect the social network characteristics, especially formation, size and diversity, to be measured later as globally expanded networks.

Second, cultural consensus analysis based on closeness/distance between cultures (Casciaro et al., 2015) can reveal further insights into cross-cultural adjustment processes for other collaborative projects under the BRI. Future studies could examine the role of high versus low cultural consensus in networking and cross-cultural adjustment. The degree of consensus/deviation between home country and host country cultural norms may influence the formation of cross-cultural networks in different ways and subsequently, would influence individual networking behaviour as well as the development of social networks in cross-cultural workplaces.

Third, it is possible to explore the concurrence of both positive (liking, competence) and negative (dislike, incompetence) ties within diverse social networks in future research (Harrigan et al., 2020; Labianca & Brass, 2006). The concurrence of positive and negative ties, also referred to as ambivalent ties, can provide interesting outcomes in different contexts (Harrigan et al., 2020). Greater negative ties over time may result in disbanding of newly developed social networks, whereas greater positive ties over time may result in the development of strong bonds between diverse social networks.

Lastly, this research is based on cross-sectional analysis. The interviews and surveys data were collected over a certain period from different respondents. Employee adjustment may change over time in the life cycle of projects. Future research could focus on different stages of a project and the type of networking present (i.e. either formal or informal). Longitudinal research over the lifetime of projects can provide a comprehensive understanding of the development of social networks and the changes in employee networking behaviour.

In summary, there are no shortcuts for emerging MNEs for effective and diverse social network development. In this regard, this research has provided some insights regarding the CPEC projects with individual and organizational challenges. However, the implications extend beyond the CPEC projects to all the BRI projects around the globe. Therefore, it is essential to encourage organizations and governments of China and other BRI participating countries to design policies conducive to project implementation and handling challenges in a timely manner. This objective requires China and other participating countries to tackle not only macro-level challenges, but also organizational- and individual-level issues in order to achieve efficient project operations and overall successful outcomes. It is hoped that this book will provide some meaningful recommendations for current and future participants in the development of the BRI projects.

References

Black, S., Gregersen, H. B., & Mendenhall, M. E. (1992). *Global assignments: Successfully expatriating and repatriating international managers.* San Francisco, CA: Jossey Bass.

Burt, R. S. (1992). *Structural holes: The social structure of competition.* Cambridge: Harvard University Press.

Burt, R. S. (2010). *Neighbour networks.* New York: Oxford University Press.

Burt, R. S., & Burzynska, K. (2017). Chinese entrepreneurs, social networks and guanxi. *Management and Organization Review, 13*(2), 22–260.

Burt, R. S., Hogarth, R. M., & Michaud, C. (2000). The social capital of French and American managers. *Organization Science, 11*(2), 123–147.

Burt, R. S., Kilduff, M., & Tasselli, S. (2013). Social network analysis: Foundations and frontiers on advantage. *Annual Review of Psychology, 64*(1), 527–547.

Casciaro, T., Barsade, S. G., Edmondson, A. C., Gibson, C. B., Krackhardt, D., & Labianca, G. (2015). The integration of psychological and network perspectives in organizational scholarship. *Organization Science, 26*(4), 1162–1176.

Chen, Y., Friedman, R., Yu, E., & Sun, F. (2009). Examining the positive and negative effects of guanxi practices: A multi-level analysis of guanxi practices and procedural justice perceptions. *Asia Pacific Journal of Management, 28*(4), 715–735.

Durbin, S. (2011). Creating knowledge through networks: A gender perspective. *Gender, Work and Organization, 18*(1), 90–112.

Granovetter, M. S. (1973). The strength of weak ties. *American Journal of Sociology, 78*(6), 1360–1380.

Gulati, R. (1998). Alliances and networks. *Strategic Management Journal, 19*, 293–317.

Gulati, R., Nohria, N., & Zaheer, A. (2000). Strategic networks. *Strategic Management Journal, 21*(3), 203–215.

Guo, Y., Rammal, H. G., Benson, J., Zhu, Y., & Dowling, P. J. (2018). Interpersonal relations in China: Expatriates' perspective on the development and use of guanxi. *International Business Review, 27*(2), 455–464.

Guo, Y., Rammal, H. G., & Pereira, V. (2021). Am I 'In or Out'? A social identity approach to studying expatriates' social networks and adjustment in a host country context. *Journal of Business Research, 136*, 558–566.

Harrigan, N., Labianca, G., & Agneessens, F. (2020). Negative ties and signed graphs research: Stimulating research on dissociative forces in social networks. *Social Networks, 60*, 1–10.

Hechanova, R., Beehr, T. A., & Christiansen, N. D. (2003). Antecedents and consequences of employees adjustment to overseas assignment: A meta-analytic review. *Applied Psychology: An International Review, 52*(2), 213–236.

Islam, N. (2004). Sifarish, sycophants, power and collectivism: Administrative culture in Pakistan. *International Review of Administrative Sciences, 70*(2), 311–330.

Labianca, G., & Brass, D. (2006). Exploring the social ledger: Negative relationships and negative asymmetry in social networks in organizations. *Academy of Management Review, 31*(3), 596–614.

Lin, N. (1999a). Building a network theory of social capital. *Connections, 22*(1), 28–51.

Lin, N. (1999b). Social networks and status attainment. *Annual Review of Sociology, 25*, 467–487.

Lin, N. (2001). *Social capital: A theory of social structure and action.* Cambridge: Cambridge University Press.

Savani, K., Morris, M. W., Naidu, N. V. R., Kumar, S., & Berlia, N. V. (2011). Cultural conditioning: Understanding interpersonal accommodation in India and the United States in terms of the modal characteristics of interpersonal influence situations. *Journal of Personality and Social Psychology, 100*(1), 84–102.

Seibert, S. E., Kraimer, M. L., & Liden, R. C. (2001). A social capital theory of career success. *The Academy of Management Journal, 44*(2), 219–237.

Soda, G., Tortoriello, M., & Iorio, A. (2018). Harvesting value from brokerage: Individual strategic orientation, structural holes, and performance. *Academy of Management Journal, 61*(3), 896–918.

Wang, X., & Nayir, D. Z. (2006). How and when is social networking important? Comparing European expatriate adjustment in China and Turkey. *Journal of International Management, 12*(4), 449–472.

Appendices

Appendix 1 – Interview Guide

Interview Guide for Social Networks and Networking in Cross-Cultural Collaborative Projects: The Case of China-Pakistan Economic Corridor (CPEC)

Section 1: Background

1. How long have you been working on this project? Can you please tell something about the project? Its duration and objectives?
2. How many people are working in your team, how many Chinese and Pakistani employees are working together?
3. Do you think national culture affects the team members working within this project? How?
4. What are the similarities and differences you have observed in the working habits of employees from other country?
5. Does the difference in national culture increases problems among team members in interaction?
6. Do different national cultures improve project efficiency?
7. Do you think language acts as barrier towards whom you know? If yes, how do you overcome this?

Section 2: Individual Cross-Cultural Interaction and Support

1. How close are you to the people in your project? Do you treat them as close friends with your nationality versus foreign nationality?
2. Do they easily accept you as part of their group among their own nationality?
3. Do you have to make an effort in order to be accepted by other nationality group?
4. What are the challenges for cross-cultural communication at workplace?

5. Do you interact with team members with other nationality outside project time, such as for a dinner, coffee or other social activities?
6. Whom do you consider as your in-group members and out-group members in this project? How do you decide if the person is from your in-group or out-group?
7. Are there any new people who have been added in your in-group since you started working on this project?
8. How the interaction with other culture has helped you in achieving better communication outcome?
9. How has the relationship (e.g. *guanxi* or *hawala*) and the current social networks helped you in your transformation? Is there the same meaning between *guanxi* and *hawala*?
10. Do you get any support from your peers and colleagues? If yes how?
11. Do you have a mentor or mentoring programme supporting people for better cross-cultural communication at workplace?
12. Do your management and administration support you through training, developing new connections and/or helping you in your adjustment to cope with cross-cultural challenges?
13. Does your project manager play an important role in handling the miscommunication and conflicts among members?
14. Do you try to meet new people from other departments/projects seek their guidance and help? Are they mostly Pakistani or Chinese?
15. When you cannot find a solution for a professional problem, whom you try to contact first? People in your network or other people outside your company (e.g. in other company, ex-colleagues)?

Section 3: Adjustment and Outcomes

1. Do you see yourself more confident, comfortable and adjusted in your work and project as compared to when you started working on it? How?
2. What major adjustments you have made in terms of developing cross-cultural networks and better communications since you joined the project?
3. Do you think these adjustments have resulted in positive outcomes for you and your project? Yes? No? Why?
4. What are those positive outcomes which have been achieved so far? (e.g. early completion, reduction of cost, less conflicts, higher productivity and so on)
5. What are the important factors determining those positive outcomes being sustainable?

Appendix 2 – Survey Questionnaires

Survey for Social Networks and Networking in Cross-Cultural Collaborative Projects: The Case of China-Pakistan Economic Corridor (CPEC)

<u>For Chinese Nationals</u>

Please list the initials of the people who have helped you in your job over the past 6–12 months. They could be colleagues, ex colleagues, friends etc.	List down the nationality of the person P= Pakistani C=Chinese O=Other	Please tick the relevant column for each of the listed initials			How close have you felt towards this person over the last 6–12 months. Please tick ONE.				How often do you contact this person? Please tick ONE.			
		Employee in same organization/ project	Employee in my previous organization	Friends and family not in same or previous organization	Very close	Close	Somewhat close	Not very close	Daily	Weekly	Monthly	Quarterly
List a maximum of 6 initials of the people who have supported you. AA (for example)	Nationality P (for example)											
1.												
2.												
3.												
4.												
5.												
6.												

The statements below describe behaviour between **colleagues. Please tick the box which best explains what you do.**

	Always	*Very often*	*Sometimes*	*Rarely*	*Never*
In my company, I approach employees I know by sight and start a conversation	Υ	Υ	Υ	Υ	Υ
I use company events to make new contacts	Υ	Υ	Υ	Υ	Υ
If I want to meet a person who could be of professional importance to me I take the initiative and introduce myself	Υ	Υ	Υ	Υ	Υ
I catch up with colleagues from other departments about what they are working on	Υ	Υ	Υ	Υ	Υ
If I can't help a colleague from another department directly, I will keep an eye out for him/her	Υ	Υ	Υ	Υ	Υ
I discuss problems with colleagues from other departments that they are having with their work	Υ	Υ	Υ	Υ	Υ
I discuss upcoming organizational changes with colleagues from other departments	Υ	Υ	Υ	Υ	Υ
When I need answers to sensitive questions I turn to reliable colleagues to find out more about the matter	Υ	Υ	Υ	Υ	Υ
At informal occasions I exchange professional tips and hints with colleagues from other departments	Υ	Υ	Υ	Υ	Υ

The following questions ask you how often you interact with **people that you know, and they work in other organizations.** These are people with whom you discuss job-related matters but **are not members of your organization. This includes people from other companies, other administrative departments, universities or other organizations.**

	Always	Very often	Sometimes	Rarely	Never
I develop informal contacts with professionals outside the organization, in order to have personal links beyond the company	Υ	Υ	Υ	Υ	Υ
I use business trips or training programmes to build new contacts	Υ	Υ	Υ	Υ	Υ
When I meet a person from another organization who could be an important business contact for me, I compare notes with him/her about our common work areas	Υ	Υ	Υ	Υ	Υ
I meet with people from other organizations outside of regular working hours	Υ	Υ	Υ	Υ	Υ
I meet with people from other organizations that could be of professional importance to me at casual get-togethers	Υ	Υ	Υ	Υ	Υ
I use business events outside of the organization (trade shows, conferences) to talk to business acquaintances on a personal level	Υ	Υ	Υ	Υ	Υ
If I meet people from other organizations, I approach them to catch up on news and changes in their professional lives	Υ	Υ	Υ	Υ	Υ
I exchange professional tips and hints with people from other organizations	Υ	Υ	Υ	Υ	Υ
I confide in people outside of the organization for job-related matters	Υ	Υ	Υ	Υ	Υ

The following questions are about how comfortable you are while working with Pakistani nationals and living in Pakistan. Indicate **how well adjusted** (how comfortable) you are to each of the following aspects of working in Pakistan?

	Very much Adjusted	Adjusted	Neutral	Not Adjusted	Very Unadjusted/ Very uncomfortable
Living conditions in general	Υ	Υ	Υ	Υ	Υ
Housing conditions	Υ	Υ	Υ	Υ	Υ
Food	Υ	Υ	Υ	Υ	Υ
Shopping	Υ	Υ	Υ	Υ	Υ
Cost of living	Υ	Υ	Υ	Υ	Υ
Entertainment/ recreation facilities and opportunities	Υ	Υ	Υ	Υ	Υ
Healthcare facilities	Υ	Υ	Υ	Υ	Υ
Socializing with Pakistani nationals	Υ	Υ	Υ	Υ	Υ
Interacting with Pakistanis on a day-to-day basis	Υ	Υ	Υ	Υ	Υ
Interacting with Pakistanis outside of work	Υ	Υ	Υ	Υ	Υ
Speaking with Pakistani nationals	Υ	Υ	Υ	Υ	Υ
Specific job responsibilities	Υ	Υ	Υ	Υ	Υ
Performance standards and expectations	Υ	Υ	Υ	Υ	Υ
Supervisory responsibilities	Υ	Υ	Υ	Υ	Υ
Safety	Υ	Υ	Υ	Υ	Υ

The following questions relate to **your work**. Indicate your responses to the level of how much you agree/disagree to:

	Strongly agree	Agree	Neutral	Disagree	Strongly Disagree
Project is able to meet the originally set project goals	Υ		Υ	Υ	Υ	Υ

(Continued)

	Strongly agree	Agree	Neutral	Disagree	Strongly Disagree	
Expected amount of work is completed as required	Υ	Υ	Υ	Υ	Υ	
High quality of work been completed	Υ	Υ	Υ	Υ	Υ	
Project/Tasks adhere to schedule (deadlines)	Υ	Υ	Υ	Υ	Υ	
Project/Tasks adhere to budget	Υ	Υ	Υ	Υ	Υ	
Project efficiency of task operations	Υ	Υ	Υ	Υ	Υ	
Systems and procedures are in place to resolve disputes among employees	Υ	Υ	Υ	Υ	Υ	
Differences in opinion with other employees is an opportunity to improve relationship effectiveness	Υ	Υ	Υ	Υ	Υ	
Settling of disputes is joint responsibility of me and organization	Υ	Υ	Υ	Υ	Υ	
There are regular discussions among peers and supervisors for any difference of opinions	Υ	Υ	Υ	Υ		Υ

The following statements are about communication in your company. **Please tick the box which indicates how satisfied you are with the communication at work**

	Strongly Agree	Agree	Neutral	Disagree	Strongly Disagree
Company/project communication motivates and stimulates an enthusiasm for meeting project goals	Υ	Υ	Υ	Υ	Υ
People in my project have great ability as communicators	Υ	Υ	Υ	Υ	Υ

(*Continued*)

	Strongly Agree	Agree	Neutral	Disagree	Strongly Disagree
Company's communication regarding project makes me identify with it or feel a vital part of it	Υ	Υ	Υ	Υ	Υ
I receive on-time information needed to do my job.	Υ	Υ	Υ	Υ	Υ
Conflicts are handled appropriately through proper communication channels.	Υ	Υ	Υ	Υ	Υ
Upper management listens and pays attention to me.	Υ	Υ	Υ	Υ	Υ
My supervisor offers guidance for solving job-related problems	Υ	Υ	Υ	Υ	Υ
My supervisor trusts me	Υ	Υ	Υ	Υ	Υ
My supervisor is open to ideas	Υ	Υ	Υ	Υ	Υ
Overall, I am satisfied with the communication taking place in my company/project	Υ	Υ	Υ	Υ	Υ

Interviewee Profile:
Please comment as appropriately

1. Gender: ☐ Female   ☐ Male

2. Current Age (in years):

3. Position/Designation (please specify):

4. What is your highest level of education:

5. Did you receive any language (English) training after joining the project?   ☐ Yes   ☐ No

6. Did you receive any language (Urdu) training after joining the project?   ☐ Yes   ☐ No

7. Do you have any previous international experience?   ☐ Yes   ☐ No

8. Company name

THANK YOU VERY MUCH FOR YOUR TIME!

If you have any comments, please feel free to comment below.

For Pakistani Nationals

Please list the initials of the people who have helped **you in your job over the past 6–12 months.** They could be colleagues, ex colleagues, friends etc.	List down the nationality of the person *P = Pakistani* *C=Chinese* *O=Other*	Please tick the relevant column for each of the listed initials		How close have you felt towards this person over the last 6–12 months. Please tick ONE.				How often do you contact this person? Please tick ONE.			
		Employee in **same** organization/ project	Employee in **my previous organization**	**Very close**	**Close**	**Somewhat close**	**Not very close**	Daily	Weekly	Monthly	Quarterly
	Nationality		**Friends and family** not in same or previous organization								
List a maximum of 6 initials of the people **who have supported** you.	P (for example)										
AA (for example)											
7.											
8.											
9.											
10.											
11.											
12.											

The statements below describe behaviour between **colleagues. Please tick the box which best explains what you do**.

	Always	Very often	Sometimes	Rarely	Never
In my company, I approach employees I know by sight and start a conversation	Υ	Υ	Υ	Υ	Υ
I use company events to make new contacts	Υ	Υ	Υ	Υ	Υ
If I want to meet a person who could be of professional importance to me I take the initiative and introduce myself	Υ	Υ	Υ	Υ	Υ
I catch up with colleagues from other departments about what they are working on	Υ	Υ	Υ	Υ	Υ
If I can't help a colleague from another department directly, I will keep an eye out for him/her	Υ	Υ	Υ	Υ	Υ
I discuss problems with colleagues from other departments that they are having with their work	Υ	Υ	Υ	Υ	Υ
I discuss upcoming organizational changes with colleagues from other departments	Υ	Υ	Υ	Υ	Υ
When I need answers to sensitive questions I turn to reliable colleagues to find out more about the matter	Υ	Υ	Υ	Υ	Υ
At informal occasions I exchange professional tips and hints with colleagues from other departments	Υ	Υ	Υ	Υ	Υ

The following questions ask you how often you interact with **people that you know and they work in other organizations**. These are people with whom you discuss job-related matters but **are not members of your organization. This includes people from other companies, other administrative departments, universities or other organizations.**

	Always	*Very often*	*Sometimes*	*Rarely*	*Never*
I develop informal contacts with professionals outside the organization, in order to have personal links beyond the company	Υ	Υ	Υ	Υ	Υ
I use business trips or training programmes to build new contacts	Υ	Υ	Υ	Υ	Υ
When I meet a person from another organization who could be an important business contact for me, I compare notes with him/her about our common work areas	Υ	Υ	Υ	Υ	Υ
I meet with people from other organizations outside of regular working hours	Υ	Υ	Υ	Υ	Υ
I meet with people from other organizations that could be of professional importance to me at casual get-togethers	Υ	Υ	Υ	Υ	Υ
I use business events outside of the organization (trade shows, conferences) to talk to business acquaintances on a personal level	Υ	Υ	Υ	Υ	Υ
If I meet people from other organizations, I approach them to catch up on news and changes in their professional lives	Υ	Υ	Υ	Υ	Υ
I exchange professional tips and hints with people from other organizations	Υ	Υ	Υ	Υ	Υ
I confide in people outside of the organization for job-related matters	Υ	Υ	Υ	Υ	Υ

The following questions are about how comfortable you are while working with Chinese nationals. Indicate **how well adjusted (how comfortable) you are to each of the following aspects of working with Chinese nationals?**

	Very much Adjusted	Adjusted	Neutral	Not Adjusted	Very Unadjusted/ Very uncomfortable
Socializing with Chinese nationals	Y	Y	Y	Y	Y
Interacting with Chinese on a day-to-day basis	Y	Y	Y	Y	Y
Interacting with Chinese outside of work	Y	Y	Y	Y	Y
Speaking with Chinese nationals	Y	Y	Y	Y	Y
Specific job responsibilities	Y	Y	Y	Y	Y
Performance standards and expectations	Y	Y	Y	Y	Y
Supervisory responsibilities	Y	Y	Y	Y	Y
Job safety and security	Y	Y	Y	Y	Y

The following questions relate to **your work. Indicate your responses to the level of how much you agree/disagree to:**

	Strongly agree	Agree	Neutral	Disagree	Strongly Disagree
Project is able to meet the originally set project goals	Y	Y	Y	Y	Y
Expected amount of work is completed as required	Y	Y	Y	Y	Y
High quality of work been completed	Y	Y	Y	Y	Y
Project/Tasks adhere to schedule (deadlines)	Y	Y	Y	Y	Y
Project/Tasks adhere to budget	Y	Y	Y	Y	Y

(*Continued*)

	Strongly agree	Agree	Neutral	Disagree	Strongly Disagree
Project efficiency of task operations	Υ	Υ	Υ	Υ	Υ
Systems and procedures are in place to resolve disputes among employees	Υ	Υ	Υ	Υ	Υ
Differences in opinion with other employees is an opportunity to improve relationship effectiveness	Υ	Υ	Υ	Υ	Υ
Settling of disputes is joint responsibility of me and organization	Υ	Υ	Υ	Υ	Υ
There are regular discussions among peers and supervisors for any difference of opinions	Υ	Υ	Υ	Υ	Υ

The following statements are about communication in your company. **Please tick the box which indicates how satisfied you are with the communication at work**

	Strongly Agree	Agree	Neutral	Disagree	Strongly Disagree
Company/project communication motivates and stimulates an enthusiasm for meeting project goals	Υ	Υ	Υ	Υ	Υ
People in my project have great ability as communicators	Υ	Υ	Υ	Υ	Υ

(*Continued*)

	Strongly Agree	Agree	Neutral	Disagree	Strongly Disagree
Company's communication regarding project makes me identify with it or feel a vital part of it	Υ	Υ	Υ	Υ	Υ
I receive on-time information needed to do my job.	Υ	Υ	Υ	Υ	Υ
Conflicts are handled appropriately through proper communication channels	Υ	Υ	Υ	Υ	Υ
Upper management listens and pays attention to me	Υ	Υ	Υ	Υ	Υ
My supervisor offers guidance for solving job-related problems	Υ	Υ	Υ	Υ	Υ
My supervisor trusts me	Υ	Υ	Υ	Υ	Υ
My supervisor is open to ideas	Υ	Υ	Υ	Υ	Υ
Overall, I am satisfied with the communication taking place in my company/project	Υ	Υ	Υ	Υ	Υ

Interviewee Profile:

Please Comment as appropriately

1. Gender: ☐ Male   ☐ Female

2. Current Age (in years):   _____

3. Position/Designation (please specify):   _____

4. What is your highest level of education: _____

5. Did you receive any language (Mandarin)   ☐ Yes   ☐ No
   training after joining the project?

6. Do you have any previous international   ☐ Yes   ☐ No
   experience?

7. Company name   _____

THANK YOU VERY MUCH FOR YOUR TIME!
If you have any comments, please feel free to comment below.

Index

Printed in the United States
by Baker & Taylor Publisher Services

Printed in the United States
by Baker & Taylor Publisher Services